Pierre Lison

Robust Processing of Spoken Situated Dialogue

A Study in Human-Robot Interaction

Diplomica® Verlag GmbH

Lison, Pierre: Robust Processing of Spoken Situated Dialogue. A Study in Human-Robot Interaction, Hamburg, Diplomica Verlag GmbH 2010

ISBN: 978-3-8366-9113-0
Druck: Diplomica® Verlag GmbH, Hamburg, 2010
Covergestaltung: Pierre Lison

Bibliografische Information der Deutschen Nationalbibliothek:
Die Deutsche Nationalbibliothek verzeichnet diese Publikation in der Deutschen Nationalbibliografie;
detaillierte bibliografische Daten sind im Internet über http://dnb.d-nb.de abrufbar.

Die digitale Ausgabe (eBook-Ausgabe) dieses Titels trägt die ISBN 978-3-8366-4113-5 und kann über den Handel oder den Verlag bezogen werden.

Dieses Werk ist urheberrechtlich geschützt. Die dadurch begründeten Rechte, insbesondere die der Übersetzung, des Nachdrucks, des Vortrags, der Entnahme von Abbildungen und Tabellen, der Funksendung, der Mikroverfilmung oder der Vervielfältigung auf anderen Wegen und der Speicherung in Datenverarbeitungsanlagen, bleiben, auch bei nur auszugsweiser Verwertung, vorbehalten. Eine Vervielfältigung dieses Werkes oder von Teilen dieses Werkes ist auch im Einzelfall nur in den Grenzen der gesetzlichen Bestimmungen des Urheberrechtsgesetzes der Bundesrepublik Deutschland in der jeweils geltenden Fassung zulässig. Sie ist grundsätzlich vergütungspflichtig. Zuwiderhandlungen unterliegen den Strafbestimmungen des Urheberrechtes.

Die Wiedergabe von Gebrauchsnamen, Handelsnamen, Warenbezeichnungen usw. in diesem Werk berechtigt auch ohne besondere Kennzeichnung nicht zu der Annahme, dass solche Namen im Sinne der Warenzeichen- und Markenschutz-Gesetzgebung als frei zu betrachten wären und daher von jedermann benutzt werden dürften.

Die Informationen in diesem Werk wurden mit Sorgfalt erarbeitet. Dennoch können Fehler nicht vollständig ausgeschlossen werden, und der Diplomica Verlag, die Autoren oder Übersetzer übernehmen keine juristische Verantwortung oder irgendeine Haftung für evtl. verbliebene fehlerhafte Angaben und deren Folgen.

© Diplomica Verlag GmbH
http://www.diplomica-verlag.de, Hamburg 2010
Printed in Germany

To Caroline

Abstract

Spoken dialogue is often considered as one of the most natural means of interaction between a human and a machine. It is, however, notoriously hard to process automatically. As many corpus studies have shown, natural spoken dialogue is replete with disfluent, partial, elided or ungrammatical utterances, all of which are very hard to accommodate in a dialogue system. Furthermore, automatic speech recognition is known to be a highly error-prone task, especially when dealing with complex, open-ended discourse domains. The combination of these two problems – ill-formed and/or misrecognised speech inputs – raises a major challenge to the development of robust dialogue systems.

This thesis presents an integrated approach for addressing these issues in the context of domain-specific dialogues for human-robot interaction. Several new techniques and algorithms have been developed to this end. They can be divided into two main lines of work.

The first line of work pertains to speech recognition. We describe a new model for *context-sensitive speech recognition* specifically suited to our application domain. The underlying hypothesis is that, in situated human-robot interaction, speech recognition performance can be significantly improved by exploiting contextual knowledge about the physical environment (objects perceived in the visual scene) and the dialogue history (previously referred-to objects within the current dialogue). The language model is dynamically updated as the environment changes, and is used to establish expectations about uttered words which are most likely to be heard given the context.

The second line of work deals with the *robust parsing of spoken inputs*. We present a new approach for this task, based on an incremental parser for Combinatory Categorial Grammar [CCG]. The parser takes word lattices as input and is able to handle ill-formed and misrecognised utterances by selectively relaxing and extending its set of grammatical rules. This operation is done via the introduction of non-standard CCG rules into the grammar. The choice of the most relevant interpretation is then realised via a discriminative model augmented with contextual information. The model includes a broad range of linguistic and contextual features, and can be trained with a simple perceptron algorithm.

All the algorithms presented in this thesis are fully implemented, and integrated as part of a distributed cognitive architecture for autonomous robots. We performed an extensive evaluation of our approach using a set of Wizard of Oz experiments. The obtained results demonstrate very significant improvements in accuracy and robustness compared to the baseline.

Zusammenfassung

Gesprochener Dialog wird oft als eines des natürlichsten Mittel der Interaktion zwischen Mensch und Maschine gesehen. Dieser ist jedoch notorisch schwer mit Sprachtechnologie zu verarbeiten. Wie viele Korpusstudien gezeigt haben, ist natürlicher, gesprochener Dialog voll von Disfluenzen, bruchstückhaften und von Auslassungen geprägten, sowie ungrammatischen Äußerungen, die alle schwer in ein Dialogsystem zu integrieren sind. Automatische Spracherkennung ist außerdem als fehlerträchtige Aufgabe bekannt, ganz besonders, wenn es um komplexe, offene Domänen geht. Das Zusammentreffen dieser beiden Probleme - fehlgeformte, und/oder falsch erkannte Spracheingaben - stellt eine große Herausforderung bei der Entwicklung von robusten Dialogsystemen dar.

Diese Arbeit stellt einen integrierten Ansatz für den Umgang mit diesen Problemen im Kontext des domänenspezifischen Dialogs für die Mensch-Roboter Interaktion dar. Neue Techniken und Algorithmen wurden dafür entwickelt. Diese können in zwei große Richtungen gegliedert werden.

Die erste Richtung betrifft die Spracherkennung. Wir beschreiben ein neues Modell für *kontextabhängige Spracherkennung*, die besonders gut für unsere Anwendungsdomäne geeignet ist. Die zu Grunde liegende Annahme ist dabei die, dass in situationsgebundener Mensch-Roboter Interaktion die Spracherkennungsleistung durch die Ausnutzung von kontextuellem Wissen über die physische Umgebung (Objekte in der visuellen Szene) und den Dialog-Verlauf signifikant verbessert werden kann. Das Sprachmodell wird dynamisch aktualisiert, sobald sich die Umgebung verändert, und wird benutzt, um Erwartungen zu formen, welche Wörter im gegebenen Kontext am wahrscheinlichsten sind.

Die zweite große Richtung ist das *robuste Parsen gesprochener Eingaben*. Wir stellen einen neuen Ansatz für dieses Problem vor, der auf einem inkrementellen Parser für Combinatory Categorial Grammar [CCG] basiert. Der Parser nimmt Wortverbände als Eingabe und ist in der Lage, mit fehlgeformten und falsch erkannten Äußerungen umzugehen, und zwar durch das gezielte Relaxieren und Erweitern seiner Regeln. Dieses wird durch die Einführung von nicht-standard CCG Regeln in die Grammatik erreicht. Die Wahl der relevantesten Interpretation wird dann durch ein diskriminatives Modell realisiert. Das Modell schließt ein weites Spektrum von Kontext- und linguistischen Merkmalen ein und kann mit einem simplen Perzeptron trainiert werden.

Alle in dieser Arbeit vorgestellten Algorithmen sind vollständig implementiert und als Teil einer verteilten, integrierten Architektur für autonome Roboter implementiert. Wir haben unseren Ansatzes mit einer Reihe von "Zauberer von Oz"-Experimenten ausführlich evaluiert. Die erzielten Resultate zeigen gegenüber der Baseline ausgesprochen signifikante Verbesserungen sowohl der Präzision, als auch der Robustheit.

Résumé

Le *dialogue oral* est souvent considéré comme un moyen d'interaction particulièrement naturel entre un homme et une machine. Son traitement automatique est cependant notoirement difficile. Comme l'ont montré de nombreuses études de corpus, le dialogue oral fourmille en effet de disfluences, d'expressions incomplètes, élidées ou agrammaticales, autant de phénomènes linguistiques difficiles à intégrer dans un système de dialogue. À cela viennent s'ajouter les problèmes de reconnaissance vocale, une technologie générant un nombre important d'erreurs, particulièrement dans le cas de domaines de discours ouverts et complexes. La combinaison de ces deux problèmes – données mal formées et/ou mal reconnues – pose un défi majeur au développement de systèmes de dialogue robustes.

Ce mémoire présente une approche intégrée de ces questions dans le cadre d'interactions hommes-robots centrées sur des domaines spécifiques. Plusieurs techniques et algorithmes ont été développés à cet effet. Ils peuvent être répartis en deux grandes sections.

La première section concerne la reconnaissance vocale. Nous décrivons un nouveau modèle de *reconnaissance vocale sensible au contexte*, spécifiquement adapté aux interactions hommes-robots. L'hypothèse sous-jacente est que, dans le cadre d'interactions situées, les performances du système de reconnaissance vocale peuvent être significativement améliorées par l'exploitation de données contextuelles relatives à l'environnement physique (objets perçus dans le champ visuel) et linguistique (entités précédemment mentionnées au cours du dialogue). Le modèle de langage est dynamiquement mis à jour au gré de l'évolution de l'environnement, et est utilisé pour établir des prévisions quant aux mots les plus probables au vu du contexte.

La deuxième section a trait à l'*analyse syntaxique de données orales*. Notre approche est fondée sur un analyseur incrémental pour Grammaires Catégorielles Combinatoires [CCG]. L'analyseur prend un treillis de mots en entrée et traite les expressions mal formées ou mal reconnues via la relaxation et l'extension sélective de son ensemble de règles grammaticales. Cette opération est réalisée grâce à l'introduction d'un ensemble de nouvelles règles CCG non-standards dans la grammaire. Le choix de l'interprétation la plus appropriée est ensuite réalisé par un modèle discriminatif. Le modèle inclut un large nombre de traits linguistiques et contextuels, et peut être paramétré à l'aide d'un simple perceptron.

La totalité des algorithmes présentés dans ce mémoire est implémentée et intégrée dans une architecture cognitive distribuée pour robots autonomes. Une évaluation détaillée (de type "Magicien d'Oz") de notre approche a été effectuée. Les résultats obtenus montrent des améliorations significatives tant au niveau de la précision que de la robustesse.

Table of contents

Abstract vii
Zusammenfassung viii
Résumé ix
Acknowledgements xv

1 Introduction   1
  1.1 Processing spoken dialogue 2
      1.1.1 The issues 2
      1.1.2 Key ideas of our approach 5
      1.1.3 Discussion and relation to previous work 6
  1.2 Human-robot interaction 9
      1.2.1 A short historical background 9
      1.2.2 Scientific relevance of HRI 11
      1.2.3 Dimensions of HRI 12
      1.2.4 Cognitive systems for HRI 13
  1.3 Considered scenarios 14
      1.3.1 Playmate scenario 15
      1.3.2 Explorer scenario 15
  1.4 Outline 16
  1.5 Contributions 17

I Background   19

2 Situated spoken dialogue   21
  2.1 Linguistic analysis of spoken dialogue 21
      2.1.1 Example from the Apollo corpus 21
      2.1.2 Theoretical analysis 25
  2.2 Language, context and human cognition 28
      2.2.1 Phylogenetic and ontogenetic origins 28
      2.2.2 Situated human language processing 29
      2.2.3 Five working hypotheses 30
  2.3 Summary of the chapter 31

3 Theoretical foundations — 33
- 3.1 Combinatory Categorial Grammar — 33
  - 3.1.1 Lexicon — 34
  - 3.1.2 Combinatory rules — 35
  - 3.1.3 Derivations — 35
- 3.2 Hybrid Logic Dependency Semantics — 36
  - 3.2.1 Hybrid logic — 36
  - 3.2.2 Encoding linguistic meaning — 39
- 3.3 Syntax-semantics interface — 40
- 3.4 Segmented Discourse Representation Theory — 42
  - 3.4.1 Dynamic semantics — 42
  - 3.4.2 Rhetorical relations — 44
  - 3.4.3 The SDRT approach in brief — 45
  - 3.4.4 Event structure — 46
- 3.5 Summary of the chapter — 46

4 Software architecture — 49
- 4.1 Global architecture — 50
  - 4.1.1 Cognitive Systems Architecture Schema — 50
  - 4.1.2 CAST: an implementation toolkit for CAS — 51
- 4.2 The communication subarchitecture — 54
  - 4.2.1 Representations — 54
  - 4.2.2 Processes — 60
- 4.3 Summary of the chapter — 66

II Approach — 69

5 Situated Speech Recognition — 71
- 5.1 Introduction to the issue — 71
- 5.2 Psycholinguistic motivation — 72
- 5.3 Salience modeling — 72
  - 5.3.1 Visual salience — 73
  - 5.3.2 Linguistic salience — 73
  - 5.3.3 Cross-modal salience model — 74
- 5.4 Lexical activation — 75
- 5.5 Language modeling — 76
  - 5.5.1 Corpus generation — 76
  - 5.5.2 Salience-driven, class-based language models — 77
- 5.6 Evaluation — 78
  - 5.6.1 Evaluation procedure — 78

	5.6.2	Results	78
	5.6.3	Analysis	80
5.7	Summary of the chapter		80

6 Robust Parsing of Spoken Dialogue — 81

- 6.1 Grammar relaxation 83
  - 6.1.1 New type-shifting rules 83
  - 6.1.2 Paradigmatic heap rules 86
  - 6.1.3 Discourse-level composition rules 87
  - 6.1.4 ASR error correction rules 87
  - 6.1.5 Control of grammar relaxation 88
- 6.2 Discriminative models for parse selection 88
  - 6.2.1 Definition of the task 89
  - 6.2.2 A distribution-free approach 89
- 6.3 Learning 91
  - 6.3.1 Training data 91
  - 6.3.2 Averaged perceptron 92
  - 6.3.3 Decoding 93
- 6.4 Features 95
  - 6.4.1 Semantic features 95
  - 6.4.2 Syntactic features 96
  - 6.4.3 Contextual features 97
  - 6.4.4 Speech recognition features 98
- 6.5 Additional extensions 99
  - 6.5.1 Incremental parse selection 99
  - 6.5.2 Max-margin classifier (SVM) 102
- 6.6 Summary of the chapter 103

III Evaluation & Conclusion — 105

7 Evaluation — 107

- 7.1 Testing data 107
- 7.2 Evaluation procedure 108
- 7.3 Types of quantitative results 108
- 7.4 Quantitative results 110
  - 7.4.1 Comparison with baseline 111
- 7.5 Discussion of results 114

8 Conclusion — 117

- 8.1 Suggestions for further research 119

IV Appendices   123

A Packing algorithm   125
     A.1 Example 125
     A.2 Data structures 128
     A.3 Pseudo-code 130

B Detailed results for parse selection   133
     B.1 Tables 133
     B.2 Figures 137
         B.2.1 Global results with all NBest hypotheses 137
         B.2.2 Detailed results for exact-match 139
         B.2.3 Detailed results for partial-match 141

C Domain-specific grammar for corpus generation   143
     C.1 Definitions 143
     C.2 Grammar specification 144

D References   163

E Index   181

Acknowledgements

The following thesis would not have been possible without the help and support of many people, which I would like to thank.

My first thanks go to my supervisors, Prof. Hans Uszkoreit and Dr. ir. Geert-Jan M. Kruijff. Their advice and guidance have been invaluable to me. I wish to express my particular gratitude to G-J, with whom I have the privilege of working for now more than two years, and who really taught me how to do research. Thank you for your constant support and encouragements, and for your patience in reading and commenting on the successive draft versions. En in de taal van Vondel: hartelijk dank voor de kans die u me hebt geboden om aan dit boeiende project mee te werken en dit onderzoek uit te voeren, voor uw nuttige suggesties, en natuurlijk voor uw interesse en vertrouwen in mijn werk!

I am also indebted to the other (past and present) members of the CoSy / CogX research group at DFKI: Hendrik Zender, Dr. Ivana Kruijff-Korbayova, Dr. Henrik Jacobsson[1], Trevor Benjamin, Sergio Roa, Raveesh Meena and Dennis Stachowicz. It has been a great pleasure to work with you!

I would also like to thank the other researchers who took part in the CoSy consortium, especially Nick Hawes and his team at the Univ. of Birmingham for their technical and software engineering expertise.

In the course of this thesis, I had the opportunity to participate in several conferences and seminars to present my ongoing research. The lively discussions we had there provided me with very useful feedback, which helped shape the content of the thesis to a great extent. I therefore wish to acknowledge my debt to the students and researchers met at LangRo, IK, StuTS, TaCoS, ECAI, ESSLLI, and at the NaTAL workshop in Nancy. Thanks for your interest in my work!

I also wish to express my gratitude to Jason Baldridge (Univ. of Texas, Austin) and Luke Zettlemoyer (MIT) for taking the time to read and comment on my thesis, and to Trevor Benjamin, Nadiya Yampolska and Sabrina Wolter for their careful proofreading.

On a more personal note, I would like to thank my family and friends for their constant support and friendship all through these two years in Saarbrücken. We had a fantastic time together, thank you for all!

And finally, my endless love and gratitude to my beloved kjære, Caroline, to whom I owe so much. Thank you for being there, for your constant support and affection, and for bringing so much joy into my life!

---

[1] who now unfortunately turned to the Dark Side of the Force (Google Zürich, that is).

"Geschrieben steht: "Im Anfang war das Wort!"
Hier stock' ich schon! Wer hilft mir weiter fort?
Ich kann das Wort so hoch unmöglich schätzen,
Ich muss es anders übersetzen,
Wenn ich vom Geiste recht erleuchtet bin.
Geschrieben steht: Im Anfang war der Sinn.
Bedenke wohl die erste Zeile,
Dass deine Feder sich nicht übereile!
Ist es der Sinn, der alles wirkt und schafft?
Es sollte stehn: Im Anfang war die Kraft!
Doch, auch indem ich dieses niederschreibe,
Schon warnt mich was, dass ich dabei nicht bleibe.
Mir hilft der Geist! Auf einmal seh' ich Rat
Und schreibe getrost: **Im Anfang war die Tat!** "

Goethe, *Faust*, 1, 3.
(Anachronistic reflections on the pivotal role played by *situated action* in language processing for human-robot interaction)

1

Introduction

In this introductory chapter, we give an overall picture of the thesis. We start by providing a brief sketch of the main research questions pursued in this thesis. What are we trying to solve? What are precisely the issues at stake? What is the general approach chosen to address them? And how does it relate to the state of the art in the field? We then proceed with a broad introduction to the field of human-robot interaction, the application area in which our work has been carried out. We describe the fundamental questions which are studied in this research field, and their connection with other areas such as robotics and cognitive science. We also present the practical scenarios we considered for our experiments. We finally close this chapter with a general outlook on the structure of this thesis, and list the contributions we have made.

Recent years have witnessed a surge of interest for service robots endowed with communicative abilities. Such robots could take care of routine tasks, in homes, offices, schools or hospitals, help disabled or mentally impaired persons, serve as social companions for the elderly, or simply entertain us. They would assist us in our daily life activities.

These robots are, by definition, meant to be deployed in *social* environments, and their capacity to interact with humans is thus a crucial factor. A natural way to perform this interaction is through *spoken dialogue*. Unfortunately, the development of technical systems able to comprehend and produce spoken dialogue is a notoriously challenging task.

This is due to several reasons. The first one resides in the difficulty of accommodating *spoken language phenomena* such as disfluencies (pauses, corrections, repetitions, etc.), elided or fragmentary utterances in a dialogue system. A second, related issue is *speech recognition*, which is known to be highly error-prone, especially when dealing with complex, open-ended discourse domains. Finally, the dialogue systems must also deal with the inherent *complexity*, *ambiguity*, and *heterogeneity* which are characteristic of unconstrained natural language.

This thesis presents an *integrated* approach for addressing these issues in the context of domain-specific dialogues for human-robot interaction [HRI]. As we will explain in the next chapters, the underlying system is based on a *hybrid* symbolic/statistical architecture, which combines fine-grained linguistic resources with statistical knowledge to achieve both *deep* and *robust* spoken dialogue comprehension.

Another key element of our approach is the central role played by *contextual information* in the interpretation process. Contextual knowledge is here defined as including both the *situated* context (objects in the visual scene, small- and large-scale qualitative spatial knowledge) and the *dialogue* context (i.e. the history of the interaction).

The next section provides an introduction to the main research questions pursued in the present thesis.

1.1 Processing spoken dialogue

We start by addressing the first important question: what are we trying to solve? What are the most important issues at stake in spoken dialogue processing?

1.1.1 The issues

The present thesis aims to address four central issues in spoken dialogue processing: (1) ill-formed inputs, (2) speech recognition errors, (3) linguistic ambiguities, and (4) extra-grammaticality.

1. Disfluencies and ill-formed inputs in spoken language

We know from everyday experience that spoken language behaves quite differently from written language. We do not speak the way we write. The difference of communicative medium plays a major role in this discrepancy. A speech stream offers for instance no possibility for "backtracking" – once something has been uttered, it cannot be erased anymore. And, contrary to written language, the production of spoken language is strongly *time-pressured*. The pauses which are made during the production of an utterance do leave a trace in the speech stream. As a consequence, spoken dialogue is replete with *disfluencies* such as filled pauses, speech repairs, corrections or repetitions [Shriberg, 1996].

A speech stream is also more difficult to segment and delimitate than a written sentence with punctuation and clear empty spaces between words. In fact, the very concepts of "words" and "sentences", which are often taken as core linguistic objects, are much more difficult to define with regard to spoken language. When we analyse spoken language, we observe a continuous speech stream, not a sequence of discrete objects. Hence the presence of many *discourse markers* in spoken dialogue, which play an important role in determining discourse structure [Kawamori *et al.*, 1996].

<small>discourse markers</small>

A final characteristic of spoken dialogue which is worth pointing out is that few spoken utterances take the form of complete sentences. The most prototypical example is the "short answer" in response to queries, but many other types of fragments or *non-sentential utterances* can be found in real dialogues [Fernández and Ginzburg, 2002]. This is mainly due to the *interactive* nature of dialogue – dialogue participants heavily rely on what has been said previously, and seek to avoid redundancies.

<small>non-sentential utterances</small>

As a result of all these factors, spoken language contains much more disfluent, partial, elided or ungrammatical utterances than written language. The question of how to *accommodate* these types of ill-formed input is a major challenge for spoken dialogue systems.

2. Less-than-perfect automatic speech recognition

A second, related problem is *automatic speech recognition* [ASR]. Speech recognition is the first step in comprehending spoken dialogue, and a very important one. For robots operating in real-world, noisy environments, and dealing with utterances pertaining to complex, open-ended domains, this step is also highly error-prone.

<small>automatic speech recognition</small>

In spite of continuous technological advances, the performance of ASR indeed remains for most tasks at least an order of magnitude worse than that of human listeners [Moore, 2007]. And contrary to human performance, ASR accuracy is usually unable to *degrade gracefully* when faced with new conditions in the environment (ambient noise, bad microphone, non-native or regional accent, variations in voice intensity, etc.) [Cole and Zue, 1997].

<small>graceful degradation</small>

This less-than-perfect performance of ASR technology seriously hinders the robustness of dialogue comprehension systems, and new techniques are needed to alleviate this problem[1].

---

[1]The speech recogniser included into our robotic platform – Nuance Recognizer v8.5 with statistical language models – yields for instance a word error rate [WER] of about 20 % when evaluated on real spoken utterances. In other words (no pun intended), more than *one word out of five* in each utterance is actually misrecognised by the system. It is

3. Lexical, syntactic and semantic ambiguities

ambiguity

Ambiguity is pervasive in natural language – at all processing levels. These ambiguities may arise either from the lexicon, the syntax, the semantics or even the pragmatics. Resolving them is a highly complex task, which, in many cases, is difficult or even impossible to perform without the use of extra-linguistic knowledge.

The ambiguity problem also arises in spoken dialogue, due e.g. to:

- *lexical ambiguities*: the word 'right' can be both a discourse marker, an adjective expressing an attitude, or a direction;

- *syntactic ambiguities*, such the PP attachment ambiguity in (1.1), where "to the left of the box" can be attached either to the verb (indicating where the ball should be taken) or to the noun 'ball' (indicating the position of the ball object).

$$\text{"take the ball to the left of the box!"} \qquad (1.1)$$

- *pragmatic ambiguities*: the utterance in (1.2) could be both a question or an indirect command:

$$\text{"could you give me the ball?"} \qquad (1.2)$$

Our spoken dialogue comprehension system therefore needs to include a component able to resolve such ambiguities with the help of linguistic and contextual information.

4. Extra-grammaticality

extra-grammaticality

Finally, the fourth problem we want to address is *extra-grammaticality*. An extra-grammatical utterance is an utterance which is seen as grammatically correct (in regard to the internalized grammar of native speakers), but which cannot be parsed with the grammar of the system. In other words, it contains linguistic constructions which are not covered in the grammar.

Ideally, a dialogue comprehension system which encounters an extra-grammatical utterance should be able to extract *partial substructures* in the absence of a full parse for the utterance.

Consider for instance the problem of interpreting the utterance (1.3):

$$\text{"robot I want you to take the red ball"} \qquad (1.3)$$

---

thus a very serious issue.

when the grammar does *not* include the syntactic construction (1.4):

$$np_{subj} \text{ want } np_{pat} \text{ to } (s\backslash np)_{event} \quad (1.4)$$

Even if it cannot get a full-scope parse for the utterance (1.3), the dialogue comprehension system should nevertheless be (ideally) able to extract as many substructures as possible, and assemble these into a common representation. In this case, it would mean recognizing "robot" as a discourse marker, followed by the construction "I want you", a preposition 'to', and finally the imperative command "take the red ball".

These substructures could then be used by the dialogue manager, either to *execute an action* (if it has enough confidence in the computed interpretation), or to trigger a *clarification request*.

clarification request

1.1.2 Key ideas of our approach

How do we go about solving these difficult issues? Here is a short summary in three points of the approach we present in this thesis:

1. *Use context* to improve the performance of ASR. We developed a new model for *context-sensitive speech recognition*, which relies on the situated and dialogue context to prime the recognition. context-sensitive speech recognition

    To this end, we first build a cross-modal *salience model* which incorporates both *visual salience* (objects in the visual scene) and *linguistic salience* (previously referred-to objects in the dialogue history). salience model

    The salience model is then used to modify, at runtime, the probabilities of the statistical language model in the speech recogniser. This way, we can dynamically adapt the language model to the environment.

    Practically, this adaptation is done by increasing the probabilities of the words which are likely to appear given the context.

2. *Relax the grammatical constraints* in order to account for spoken language phenomena. This is done by inserting a set of *non-standard rules* to the CCG grammar. grammar relaxation

    We included new rules to handle disfluencies, missing words, slightly non-grammatical constructions, utterances combining several independent discourse units, and frequent speech recognition errors.

3. Apply a *discriminative model* on the resulting set of parses. The com- discriminative model

bined use of (1) multiple speech recognition hypotheses and (2) grammar relaxation techniques, associated to (3) the natural ambiguity inherent to language, has for consequence a substantial increase in the number of possible interpretations.

We therefore need a way to filter the set of interpretations/parses, based on their likelihood. To this end, we use a discriminative model which incorporates a large set of linguistic and contextual features, and yields a *score* to each interpretation.

The interpretation with the highest score can then be selected and transferred for further processing.

This approach has been fully implemented and integrated into a cognitive architecture for HRI. It is able to address, at least partially, the four issues we just mentioned regarding spoken dialogue: ill-formed inputs, speech recognition errors, linguistic ambiguities, and extra-grammaticality. Experimental results on a "Wizard of Oz" test suite demonstrate the effectiveness of our approach, with very significant improvements both in *accuracy* and *robustness* (**55.6** % increase in the exact-match accuracy of the final chosen interpretation over the baseline performance).

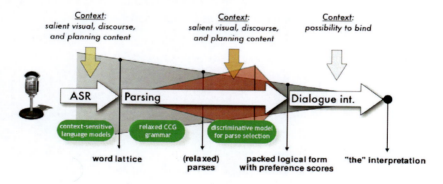

Figure 1.1: Processing workflow for robust spoken dialogue comprehension.

1.1.3 Discussion and relation to previous work

There are three defining characteristics of our approach we would like to stress:

hybrid approach

1. It is a *hybrid* symbolic/statistical approach to spoken dialogue pro-

cessing. The implemented mechanisms combine fine-grained linguistic resources (the CCG lexicon) with statistical information (the ASR language model and the discriminative model). The resulting system therefore draws from the best of both worlds and is able to deliver both *deep* and *robust* language processing.

2. It is also an *integrated* approach to spoken dialogue comprehension. It goes all the way from the signal processing of the speech input up to the logical forms and the pragmatic interpretation. The various components involved in dialogue processing interact with each other in complex ways to complement, coordinate and constrain their internal representations.

   integration

3. And finally, it is also a *context-sensitive* approach. Contextual information is used at each processing step, either as an *anticipatory* mechanism (to guide expectations about what is likely to be uttered next), or as a *discriminative* mechanism (to prune interpretations which are contextually unlikely). These mechanisms are implemented by the dynamic adaptation of the ASR language model and the use of contextual features in the discriminative model for robust parsing.

   context-sensitivity

The question to address now is: how does our approach compare to the state of the art in robust processing of spoken dialogue?

Commercial spoken dialogue systems traditionally rely on *shallow parsing* techniques such as *"concept spotting"*. In this approach, a small hand-crafted, task-specific grammar is used to extract specific constituents, such as locative phrases or temporal expressions, and turn these into basic semantic concepts [Ward, 1989; Jackson *et al.*, 1991; Aust *et al.*, 1995; Dowding *et al.*, 1994; Allen *et al.*, 1996]. These techniques are usually very efficient, but also present several important shortcomings, as they are often highly domain-specific, fragile, and require a lot of development and optimisation effort to implement.

shallow parsing

In more recent years, several new techniques emerged, mainly based on statistical approaches. In the CHORUS system [Pieraccini *et al.*, 1992], the utterances are modeled as *Hidden Markov Models* [HMMs], in which hidden states correspond to semantic concepts and the state outputs correspond to the individual words.

Hidden Markov Models

HMMs are a *flat-concept* model – the semantic representation is just a linear sequence of concepts with no internal structure. To overcome this problem, various *stochastic parsing* techniques have been proposed, based either on *Probabilistic Context Free Grammars* [Miller *et al.*, 1994; Fine,

stochastic parsing

7

1998], *lexicalised models* [Collins, 1997; Charniak, 2001], *data-oriented parsing* [Bod, 1999; Sima'an, 2004], or *constrained hierarchical models* [He and Young, 2005]. A few recent systems, such as the SOUP parser, also attempt to combine shallow parsing with statistical techniques, based on a hand-crafted grammar associated with probabilistic weights [Gavaldà, 2004].

More rarely, we can also find in the literature some descriptions of spoken dialogue systems performing a real *grammatical analysis*, usually along with a "robustness" mechanism to deal with speech recognition errors, extra-grammaticality [van Noord *et al.*, 1999; Chanod, 2000] or ill-formed inputs [Zettlemoyer and Collins, 2007].

<!-- margin: grammatical analysis -->

Compared to the state of the art, our approach is unique in the sense that it is, to the best of our knowledge, the only one which attempts to combine *deep* grammatical analysis together with *statistical* discriminative models exploiting both *linguistic* and *contextual* information.

We believe that the strategy we propose in this thesis has decisive advantages over purely shallow, statistical or symbolic methods:

- Using a deep processing approach, we are able to extract full, detailed semantic representations, which can then be used to draw inferences and perform sophisticated dialogue planning. This is not possible with shallow or statistical methods.

- At the same time, due to the grammar relaxation mechanism and the discriminative model, we do not suffer from the inherent fragility of purely symbolic methods. Our parsing method is particularly robust, both to speech recognition errors and to ill-formed utterances.

- Finally, contrary to "concept spotting" techniques, our approach is much less domain-specific: the parser relies on a general-purpose lexicalised grammar which can be easily reused in other systems.

Our approach is also original in its tight *integration* of multiple knowledge sources – and particularly contextual knowledge sources – all through the utterance comprehension process. Many dialogue systems are designed in a classical modular fashion, where the output of a component serves as direct input for the next component, with few or no interactions other than this pipelined exchange of data[2]. Our strategy, however, is to put the tight, multi-level integration of *linguistic* and *contextual* information at the very center of processing.

---

[2] Some interesting exceptions to this design include integrated approaches such as [Moore *et al.*, 1995; Gabsdil and Bos, 2003].

As a final note, we would like to stress that our dialogue comprehension system also departs from previous work in the way we define "context". Many recent techniques have been developed to take context into account in language processing (see e.g. Gruenstein *et al.* [2005]). But the vast majority of these approaches take a rather narrow view of context, usually restricting it to the mere dialogue/discourse context. Our dialogue comprehension system is one of the only ones (with the possible exceptions of Roy [2001]; Chai and Qu [2005]; Gorniak and Roy [2007]) to define context in a *multimodal* fashion, with a special focus on *situated context*.

In the next section, we describe the field of Human-Robot Interaction, the application area in which our work has been implemented and evaluated.

1.2 Human-robot interaction

How can we make talking robots? That is, how can we develop robots capable of interacting with humans using natural languages like English or German? How can we make them understand dialogue – more specifically, how can we make them understand *situated, spoken* dialogue? And what's more, how do we enable them to go beyond mere "understanding" and be able to actively *participate* in a dialogue, by contributing to the interaction in a meaningful and contextually relevant way?

situated spoken dialogue

These questions are at the core of an emerging research field called **human-robot interaction**, or HRI. Human-robot interaction is the field of study dedicated to understanding, designing, and evaluating robotic systems for use by or with humans [Goodrich and Schultz, 2007]. Interaction, by definition, requires communication between robots and humans. The basic goal of HRI is to develop principles, techniques and algorithms to allow for *natural* and *effective* communication between humans and robots. As one might expect, HRI is a highly *multidisciplinary* research area, drawing from a wide range of fields such as artificial intelligence, engineering, robotics, (computational) linguistics, cognitive science, social psychology, human factors engineering and design, and anthropology.

human-robot interaction

1.2.1 A short historical background

The concept of "robot" as a mechanical creature working for (and sometimes against) humans has been around for centuries in religion, mythology, philosophy, and fiction[3]. The word "robot" itself originates from the Czech word

---

[3]In the *Iliad*, written around 800 BC, Homer describes some of the creatures crafted by Hephaistos (the god of forge and fire) as "golden handmaids" looking like real persons, with

robota, which means drudgery or servitude. It appears to have first been used in Karel Chapek's 1920's play *Rossum's Universal Robots*.

The development of modern-day robotics went hand in hand with the emergence of electronics, and the first real implementations can be traced back to the early 70s. One of the most famous engineering example of this period is the autonomous "Shakey" robot, which could navigate in a small block world. and move different kinds of objects [Nilsson, 1984].

Figure 1.2: Shakey the robot

sense-plan-act

behaviour-based robotics

Robots such as Shakey are based on a centralised architecture operating under a monolithic *sense-plan-act* loop. This kind of architecture suffers from a number of key problems in terms of robustness and adaptation [Brooks, 1986], and in the mid-eighties, a new alternative paradigm started to emerge, called *behaviour-based robotics*.

In this paradigm, behaviour is designed from the "bottom-up", based on a set of autonomy modules mapping sensors directly to actions, with few or no internal representation. These modules are then integrated to create an *emergent* system [Arkin, 1998; Brooks, 1986, 1999].

sense, reason, voice and strength (Book XVIII, verse 415). In other words, Hephaistos' "handmaids" are artificial systems designed to accomplish specific tasks, and endowed with capacities for perception, reasoning, interaction and physical action – the exact definition of modern "talking robots".

Today, many robotic architectures are based on a *hybrid* combination of both approaches. These systems rely on sense-think-act models on top of a behaviour-based substrate [Murphy, 2000]. The low-level reactivity is therefore separated from higher level reasoning such as planning, reasoning, and learning [Bonasso et al., 1995].

What about human-robot interaction? For a long time, the development of HRI has been slowed down by technological constraints. The earliest types of interaction were mainly teleoperation and supervisory control [Sheridan, 1992]. In the 80s, human-robot interaction based on spoken dialogue began to emerge, usually relying on some SHRDLU-like dialogue processing scheme [Winograd, 1976]. These interactions were usually very rigid and made little use of the situated context, let alone dynamically react to it.

Progressively, the field moved towards more flexible and context-sensitive types of interaction, where the dialogue system is directly *grounded* in action and perception [Hsiao and Mavridis, 2003; Roy, 2005]. Human-robot interaction also benefited a lot from the recent technological advances in speech recognition [Gruenstein et al., 2005; Moore, 2007] and in robust natural language processing [Allen et al., 1996; Pineau et al., 2003].

grounding

1.2.2 Scientific relevance of HRI

Why is human-robot interaction an interesting and relevant topic of research? What can we exactly learn from it? Our view is that the scientific study of the inner mechanisms of human-robot interaction is important from both a *theoretical* and *practical* perspective:

Theoretical interest

The theoretical interest of HRI lies in the insights that this research area can provide about the nature of human cognition, and more specifically about the nature of human language comprehension and production.

As human beings, we learned from a very early age how to interact socially with others. And we all know that conducting a natural dialogue in a real setting requires much more than just being able to manipulate linguistic forms – may it be speech signals, words, utterances, or discourse segments. Crucially, we also need to figure out how the dialogue *relates to the world* we live in, and how it can be used as a medium for *action* and *inter-action* to help us achieve particular goals in our environment.

human language processing

That is where the study of human-robot interaction has an explanatory power which is lacking in other types of interaction. Human-robot interaction is by definition always *situated* in physical environments, and instanti-

situated context

ated ("embodied") in robotic platforms. From the perspective of Artificial Intelligence as an "experimental model" for human cognition[4], human-robot interaction can help us investigate issues concerning the cognitive plausibility of various theories in human language processing[5]. (It should however be added that a large part of the research done in HRI is application-oriented and not really directly concerned by issues of cognitive modeling).

Practical interest

service robots

HRI is also a topic of critical technological importance. The development of service robots endowed with communicative capabilities is a major area of R&D funding in the technological industry. And there is a rapidly growing body of academic research devoted to this topic as well.

This is not surprising – potential applications of such technology abound and may have a large impact in our lives. In the future, service robots could be used in domains such as domestic or hospital care, entertainment, educational or therapeutic toys, military defense, autonomous exploration, search-and-rescue operations, and space robotics – to cite just a few.

1.2.3 Dimensions of HRI

Depending on the nature of the interaction and of its participants, human-robot interactions can take very different forms. The following dimensions can be used for analysing particular instances of HRI:

1. *Remote* vs. *situated* character of the interaction;

2. Level of *autonomy* (tele-operated vs. fully autonomous systems, with mixed-initiative interactions);

3. *Communication medium* (touchscreen, keyboard terminal, speech);

4. *Unimodal* vs. *multimodal* character of the interaction;

5. *Format* of the communication (scripted language vs. free dialogue);

---

[4]Note that this doesn't mean that robots must incorporate the same "wetware" (i.e. the same brain circuitry and neuronal connections) as human beings. What is important here is to include the same cognitive *functions* as humans. The robot must be capable of "mimicking" at the functional level certain aspects of human social behaviour in order for a human to recognise it as a goal-directed, intentional agent. Its cognitive architecture should therefore reflect some level of *"functional biomimetism"*.

[5]see e.g. [Staudte and Crocker, 2008] concerning eye gaze.

6. *Duration* and *complexity* of the interaction (short-lived or covering a large number of turns);

7. Type of *task* that must be accomplished by the robot;

8. *Goal* of the interaction (i.e. information gathering, entertainment, mentoring, or collaboration to achieve a specific task).

9. Possibilities for *learning* and *adaptation*;

For the purpose of this thesis, we'll focus on the particular subset of interactions which are (1) *situated*, (2) *mixed-initiative*, and (3) based on *natural spoken dialogue*.

Figure 1.3: Example of multimodal social interaction including voice, gesture and eye gaze: the Leonardo robot from MIT [Thomaz, 2006].

Many other types of interactions exist. In industrial and commercial settings, the dominant communication media remain touchscreens, tele-operating devices and keyboard terminals. These types of interface are nevertheless far less interesting from the perspective of computational linguistics. As a consequence, we will not treat them directly in this thesis, in order to concentrate on situated spoken dialogue.

1.2.4 Cognitive systems for HRI

Robots used in HRI must generally operate in *open-ended environments* and interact with humans using *natural language* to perform a variety of service-oriented tasks.

Developing *cognitive systems* for such robots remains a formidable challenge. Software architectures for cognitive robots are typically composed of a large number of cooperating subsystems, such as communication, computer

cognitive systems

vision, navigation and manipulation skills, and various deliberative processes such as symbolic planners [Langley *et al.*, 2005].

The interactions between the various components of these architectures are often highly complex. Equipping the robot with basic functionalities for dialogue comprehension and production is not enough to make it interact naturally in situated dialogues. For a robot to be able to interact with a human, it must also build and maintain an awareness of it immediate *physical environment*, as well as of the *communicative goals and intentions* of its interlocutor, and the "possibilities for action" provided by the environment – that is, the existing *affordances*.

affordances

Cognitive systems for HRI need to find meaningful ways to relate *language, action* and *situated reality*, and enable the robot to use its rich perceptual experience to continuously learn and adapt itself to its environment, and more generally to the *context* surrounding him.

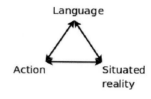

situated context

This is no trivial or secondary task. In fact, one of the central claims of this thesis is that the connection between language and situated context, far from being a minor post-processing step, is absolutely essential and pivotal to both dialogue comprehension and production. This has been known for quite some time in the psycholinguistic community (see for instance [Knoeferle and Crocker, 2006]), but has been to our knowledge scarcely applied in practical NLP systems, with a few notable exceptions that we shall discuss later.

The key insight of our approach is therefore to put context *first*, at the centre of processing, not the periphery. Context should be the very ground on which we build and maintain linguistic interpretations. We will detail in the next chapters how this insight can be exploited and put into practice for the development of a robust spoken dialogue comprehension system.

1.3 Considered scenarios

scenarios

The work done in this thesis has been conducted within practical "scenarios" of human-robot interaction. These scenarios were part of the research effort pursued during the "CoSy" project, an EU-funded Integrated Project which ran from 2004 to 2008, and carried out by a consortium of seven universities[6]. We briefly present below the two scenarios we considered in our experiments.

---

[6]see the project website for more information: http://www.cognitivesystems.org

1.3.1 Playmate scenario

The *"Playmate"* scenario, illustrated in Figure 1.4, is an object manipulation scenario. The experiments are carried out with a robotic arm combined with various cameras. The robot is able to manipulate objects, learn about their properties, and do so in conjunction with humans.

<small>object manipulation</small>

Research topics within this scenario include object categorization, spatial reference resolution, planning of high and low level actions, cross-modal learning of visual qualities, and recognition of intentional human actions[7] [Hawes *et al.*, 2009b; Brenner *et al.*, 2007; Skočaj *et al.*, 2007].

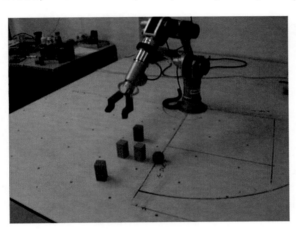

Figure 1.4: The Playmate scenario: object manipulation and visual learning.

1.3.2 Explorer scenario

The *"Explorer"* scenario, illustrated in Figure 1.5, involves a mobile robot equipped with a laser scanner and various cameras. This autonomous robot can acquire a spatial understanding of its environment, interact with humans using spoken dialogue, and search for objects in indoor environments.

<small>spatial understanding</small>

Research topics within this scenario include SLAM (Simultaneous Localization and Mapping), multi-level conceptual spatial representations, human augmented mapping (ie. the acquisition of qualitative spatial knowledge with the help of a human), visual place recognition, and object search & localisation[8] [Zender *et al.*, 2008; Sjö *et al.*, 2008].

---

[7]cf. http://www.cognitivesystems.org/playmate.asp for details.
[8]cf. http://www.cognitivesystems.org/explorer.asp for details.

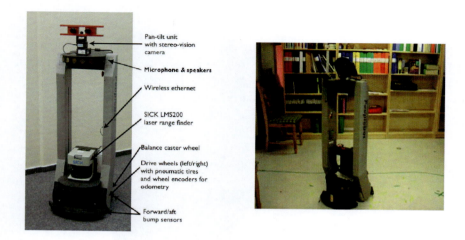

Figure 1.5: The Explorer scenario: an indoor mobile robot.

1.4 Outline

To conclude this introductory chapter, we provide a general outlook on the remaining chapters. The thesis is divided in three main parts: Background, Approach, and Evaluation & Conclusion.

- The **Background** part contains three chapters. The first chapter provides an analysis of spoken dialogue phenomena, based on corpus studies, insights from theories of natural language syntax, and experimental findings in psycholinguistics and cognitive neuroscience. The second chapter is devoted to the theoretical foundations of our work: we present the various formalisms used to represent information at the syntactic, semantic and pragmatic levels. Finally, the third chapter details the software architecture in which our system has been developed. We describe the various components and their interaction.

- In the **Approach** part, we dive into the details of our approach. The first chapter describes the model for context-sensitive speech recognition that we developed. The second chapter details the strategy we devised to handle robust parsing – that is, the grammar relaxation mechanism associated to a discriminative model.

- The **Evaluation & Conclusion** is the last part of the thesis, where we present our results. We first explain the experimental setup, then present the quantitative results, and analyse them in detail. And finally, we conclude this thesis by recapitulating what has been achieved, and what still lies ahead.

In the appendices, you will find the detailed specification of the "packing algorithm", the detailed figures and graphs for the experiments, the specifications of the domain-specific grammar used for generating the training examples, and of course the bibliography and the index.

1.5 Contributions

The thesis makes the following contributions:

1. A new model for *context-sensitive speech recognition*, which relies on the situated and dialogue context to dynamically adapt the language model of the speech recogniser to the environment;

2. A new model for *robust parsing of spoken inputs*, based on a relaxed CCG grammar combined with a discriminative model exploring a wide range of linguistic and contextual features.

3. A fully working *implementation* for these two models, integrated into a cognitive architecture for autonomous robots. The implementation comes along with a complete set of training and testing data.

The work performed for this thesis has given rise to a number of peer-reviewed publications and research talks at international conferences, which are listed on the author's website: http://www.dfki.de/~plison

The source code for the implementation is released under a GPL open-source license, along with the accompanying documentation.

Part I

Background

2
Situated spoken dialogue

This chapter is devoted to the empirical analysis of situated spoken dialogue. It is divided into two parts: the first part is a linguistic analysis of spoken interactions. As a motivating example, we present a dialogue transcript extracted from a corpus of spoken dialogue interactions, and analyse it in detail. We then give a more theoretical account of spoken dialogue phenomena, informed by linguistic theories of spoken language. The second part is devoted to the cognitive grounding of spoken situated dialogue. Based on experimental studies in psycholinguistics and cognitive neuroscience, we highlight some important findings regarding human language processing and its relation to situated awareness and possibilities for embodied action.

2.1 Linguistic analysis of spoken dialogue

In the introductory chapter, we claimed that spoken language differs fundamentally from written language along several dimensions. What are exactly these differences, and what makes them difficult to process using standard NLP tools? The next pages are devoted to answering these questions. And to make our discussion more concrete, we start with a motivating example, which will help us introduce a few important ideas.

2.1.1 Example from the Apollo corpus

The dialogue transcript shown on Table 2.1 is an excerpt from a real-life interaction between three astronauts during the Apollo 17 space mission (the last manned moon landing to date, launched on December 7, 1972). The interaction takes place at Geology Station 3, Ballet Crater.

The full transcript along with the audio file (in MP3 format) is available online[1]. The reader is invited to listen to the audio file in parallel to reading the dialogue transcript, as it will provide a clearer understanding of the various linguistic phenomena we are dealing with in this chapter.

Dialogue annotation

Here are the conventions we followed to transcribe and annotate the dialogue (based on Bachy *et al.* [2004]):

- *Short silent pauses* are indicated by one slash /, and *longer pauses* (lasting more than one second) by two slashes //;

- *Speech errors*, usually followed by their corresponding speech repairs, are indicated by a slash where the error is made, such as in ⑥: "abo/ about one left bob";

- *Filled pauses* are expressed by their usual transcriptions in English: 'uh', 'er', 'um', etc.

- *Speech overlaps* (i.e. when two or more speakers are speaking at the same time) are bracketed by ⊢ and ⊣.

- Finally, no punctuation is added to the transcript. Such punctuation would be necessarily artificial since we are dealing with spoken dialogue, where punctuation is – by definition – nonexistent.

Analysis

The transcript in Table 2.1 illustrates several important spoken dialogue phenomena, which are worth reviewing in some detail.

pauses

1. The first phenomenon we can observe is the omnipresence of *filled* and *unfilled pauses*. This is partly due to the nature of the communication medium itself – contrary to written language, speech is strongly *time-pressured*, and the hesitations made during utterance production leave a trace in the speech stream.

    But there's more. In turn-taking conversations, these disfluencies have a broad range of linguistic functions of their own. They can be used to implicate that the speaker is searching for a word, deciding what to say next, wants to keep the floor, or cede it [Clark and Fox, 2002]. They

---

[1] At the following URL: http://history.nasa.gov/alsj/a17/a17.trvsta4.html.

Schmitt :	i got your gnomon	[1]
Cernan :	sun shadow is zero	[2]
	pitch / if i can get it over to read it	[3]
	pitch is uh // pitch is zero //	[4]
	roll is zero	[5]
	abo/ about one left bob	[6]
Parker :	okay copy	[7]
	and ⊢ how about	[8]
Cernan :	about one ⊣ left	[9]
Parker :	and how about heading	[10]
Cernan :	he/ / heading is two eight two	[11]
Parker :	okay go ahead and park	[12]
	we'll give you an update when you get done //	[13]
Cernan :	what else do you need	[14]
Parker :	that's all we need	[15]
	go ahead and park ⊢ on your ⟨Schmitt⟩ okay ⊣ zero four five	[16]
	we'll give you an update when you're done	[17]
Cernan :	Jack is worth coming right there	[18]
Schmitt :	err looks like a pretty go/ good location	[19]
Cernan :	okay	[20]
Schmitt :	we can sample the rim materials of this crater //	[21]
	Bob i'm at the uh / south uh	[22]
	let's say east-southeast rim / of a uh //	[23]
	oh / thirty meter crater // err	[24]
	in the light mantle of course /	[25]
	up on the uh / Scarp and maybe // three hundred	[26]
	err two hundred meters from the uh rim of Lara	[27]
	in (*inaudible*)	[28]
	northeast direction	[29]
Parker :	okay i copy ⊢ that	[30]
Schmitt :	it ⊣ it probably shows up as a	[31]
	bright ⊢ crater ⟨**Parker**⟩ (*inaudible*) that ⊣	[32]
	a bright crater on your map	[33]
	there's only about a half a centimeter of gray cover /	[34]
	over very white material //	[35]
	uh that forms the rim	[36]

Table 2.1: Transcript excerpt from a spoken dialogue interaction between three astronauts in the Apollo 17 space mission. The full transcript (along with the audio file and additional comments) is available at this address: [http://history.nasa.gov/alsj/a17/a17.trvsta4.html]. The transcript annotation is ours.

also have a role in information structure [Arnold et al., 2003] and can serve as markers for discourse structure [Swerts et al., 1996].

repetitions

2. Some words are *repeated* several times. These repetitions can occur for various reasons. In [3]-[4] the word 'pitch' is repeated because of the introduction of a new discourse unit breaking the initial utterance, which has therefore to be started anew. In [31], the pronoun 'it' is repeated because of a speech overlap with another speaker.

corrections

3. Several *corrections* occur in the dialogue. These corrections are sometimes due to factual errors which need to be corrected, as in [26]-[27]. At other places, the correction is used to clarify or make precise what has just been said, such as in [32]-[33].

speech overlaps

4. *Speech overlaps* are far from uncommon. They are usually quite short, generally a few hundreds milliseconds of overlap between two turns (like in [30]-[31]), and often due to back-channels (cf. [16]). But longer overlaps are also possible, such as in [32], where a rather long overlap causes the first speaker to start his whole phrase anew.

back-channels

5. The transcribed dialogue presents many instances of *acknowledgements*, *back-channels* and *clarifications*. (see for instance [1], [7], [16], [32]). These dialog acts are known to be crucial for social interactions [Jurafsky et al., 1998].

speech repairs

6. The dialogue also illustrates at several places (for instance in [6] and [11]) the presence of *speech errors*, directly followed by their corresponding *speech repairs*.

non-sentential utterances

7. Many utterances found in the transcribed dialogue are *non-sentential*. They can take the form of short answers or acknowledgements ([7], [20]), utterance fragments (as in [9]), or elided utterances ([10]).

8. Several discourse units are *interrupted* by the introduction of a new discourse unit. See for instance [3], where the speaker interrupts his initial utterance for an aside comment.

9. As in all spoken dialogues, some speech segments can be *acoustically difficult to recognise* (see [28] and [32]), either because of technical problems in the communication medium, or due to other problems such as speech overlaps, pronunciation errors, low voice intensity, etc.

10. Finally, several utterances in the dialogue are *agrammatical*, at least from a normative point of view. This is often due to a missing word.

In [6], what the speaker actually means is: "about one [degree] left, Bob".
In [18], the pronoun is missing: "Jack is [it] worth coming right there".

2.1.2 Theoretical analysis

In section 1.1, we explained that one of the most important issues in spoken dialogue processing is the difficulty of accommodating in a dialogue system *spoken language phenomena* such as disfluencies, utterance fragments, or slightly agrammatical expressions.

The first step in tackling these problems is to elaborate a *linguistic analysis* of these phenomena. Once the analysis is made, it can then be *formalised* in a computational model, and ultimately serve as the basis for a practical *mechanism* implemented in the dialogue comprehension system to handle these phenomena (which is the topic of section 6.1).

So the first question we need to answer is the following: is it possible to provide a linguistic account for these spoken dialogue phenomena, possibly in a unified framework?

There is a considerable body of work devoted to this topic, which spans several decades of research in theoretical linguistics, more specifically in conversation analysis, theories of spoken language syntax and semantics, and in dialogue modeling[2].

In this section, we describe one possible analysis of spoken language, concentrating on the *syntactic treatment of disfluencies*. We leave out other interesting aspects of spoken dialogue such as the semantics and pragmatics of conversation, which are extensively discussed in the literature.

Blanche-Benveniste *et al.* [1990] offer an interesting perspective on the linguistic analysis of spoken language, based on an extensive corpus study of spoken French transcripts. Their analysis has been recently extended and formalised in works such as [Guénot, 2006], which distinguishes two types of syntactic relations: *syntagmatic* relations and *paradigmatic*[3] relations.

---

[2]Seminal papers on this topic include (with no claim to exhaustivity): [Sacks *et al.*, 1974; Grice, 1975; Searle, 1975; Power, 1979; Allen and Perrault, 1980; Grosz and Sidner, 1980; Clark and Schaefer, 1989; Goodwin, 1996; Purver *et al.*, 2001; Ginzburg, 2009].

[3]Although it is used here in a somewhat different way, the adjective "paradigmatic" is a reference to the "paradigmatic axis" of de Saussure [1949] – a concept also used later by Hjelmslev [1974] and Jakobson [1976]. In his famous course, de Saussure distinguishes two possible types of relations between signs: *syntagmatic* relations (connections between elements of the speech chain) and *paradigmatic* relations (class of linguistic elements with similarities). In the structuralist perspective of de Saussure, each language is a complex system based on relations of *difference* which place signs in opposition to one another.

Paradigmatic heaps

Syntagmatic constructions are primarily characterized by *hypotactic* (i.e. head-dependent) relations between their constituents, whereas paradigmatic ones do not have such head-dependent asymmetry. Two important families of linguistic phenomena which are generally troublesome for syntacticians can be conveniently analysed as instances of paradigmatic relations: *disfluencies* and *coordinations*.

paradigmatic heap Together, constituents connected by such paradigmatic relations form what Blanche-Benveniste *et al.* [1990] call a *"paradigmatic heap"*. A paradigmatic heap is defined as the position in a utterance where the "syntagmatic unfolding is interrupted", and the same syntactic position hence occupied by several linguistic objects.

A few examples

To make this more concrete, consider the example given in (2.1)[4]. This utterance contains several hard-to-process disfluencies. The linguistic analysis of this example is illustrated in (2.2) on two dimensions, the horizontal dimension being associated to the syntagmatic axis, and the vertical dimension to the paradigmatic axis. The disfluencies are indicated in bold characters.

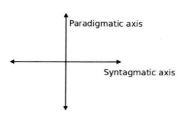

(2.1) "il il a quand même un une fibre pédagogique assez assez euh enfin réelle quoi"
"he does have a real pedagogical streak, you know"

(2.2)
    il
    il a quand même   **un**
                              une fibre pédagogique   **assez**
                                                           assez euh enfin réelle quoi

As we observe in (2.2), the disfluencies are grouped in paradigmatic heaps, represented in vertical columns. The disfluencies are "stalled" on the same syntactic position.

The utterance presented in (2.3) is another example, containing a speech repair. The associated analysis is given in (2.4).

---

[4]The examples are drawn from the *Corpus d'Interactions Dilogiques* [Bertrand and Priego-Valverde, 2005]

(2.3) "s'il n'y a pas d'éléments à mon avis euh il il tombe dans la paran/ dans la parano quoi"
"if there are no facts [backing him], I think he's falling into paranoia"

(2.4)
s'il n'y a pas d'éléments à mon avis euh **il**
            il tombe **dans la paran/**
                 dans la parano quoi

An interesting advantage of this descriptive approach is that the same conceptual toolbox can be applied to analyse coordination phenomena, such as in (2.5). The corresponding analysis is given in (2.6).

(2.5) "il y a des conflits soit des conflits d'intérêts soit des gens qui savent pas que tu es là"
"there are conflicts, either conflicts of interests, or people who don't know you're there"

(2.6)
il y a   des conflits
  soit des conflits d'intérêts
  soit des gens qui savent pas que tu es là

Application to the Apollo transcript

The analysis we just described can be conveniently applied to the problematic utterances in our Apollo transcript. We provide below analyses for three excerpts containing difficult, hard-to-process disfluencies.

(2.7)
Bob i'm at the   uh
        south uh
    let's say east-southeast rim of a uh oh
                  thirty-meter crater

(2.8)
up on the uh
    Scarp and maybe three hundred
          err two hundred meters

(2.9)
it
it probably shows up as a bright crater
           a bright crater on your map

Practical implementation

The concept of "paradigmatic heap" we just described is implemented in our approach (although in a rather limited and obviously perfectible way) via the introduction of new combinatory rules which allow constituents of the same syntactic category to be combined in order to form a "heap" (cf. section 6.1.1). The generalisation of such technique to handle the full range of paradigmatic relations is left open to future research.

2.2 Language, context and human cognition

As we said in the introductory chapter, one of the central claims of this thesis is that the connection between language and situation awareness is absolutely crucial for dialogue comprehension and production. In this section, we examine why it is so, and what lessons we can learn from these observations regarding the development of our dialogue system.

So why is situated context so important? Cognitive science offers an interesting perspective on this question, which can help shed some light into the nature of language itself. Language is indeed a cultural product deeply rooted in the specifics of human cognition. And as many cognitive scientists and philosophers have argued, human cognition must be primarily understood as an *embodied* and *situated activity*[5] (emphasis should be put on all three) rather than a formal system operating on abstract symbols. Human language processing is in this respect no different than other cognitive activities such as visuospatial attention, perception or motor control.

2.2.1 Phylogenetic and ontogenetic origins

This should not come as a surprise from an evolutionary point of view. The biological and (most importantly) cultural capacities of modern human communication didn't emerge "out of the blue", as an isolated system. It grew out of animal capacities because they proved to be instrumental in the species

---

[5]See [Anderson, 2003] for a comprehensive guide to the field of embodied and situated cognition. Foundational works in this area, ranging from many different fields (cognitive psychology, linguistics, artificial intelligence and robotics, social sciences, neurosciences), include [Lakoff and Johnson, 1980; Steels, 1994; Berthoz, 1997; Lakoff and Johnson, 1999; Brooks, 1999; Clark, 1999; Barsalou, 1999; Dourish, 2001; Wilson, 2002; Fauconnier and Turner, 2003; Roy and Reiter, 2005]. More philosophical considerations on the "embodied mind" and its relation to general semiotics and phenomenology are also worth reading, see in particular [Heidegger, 1927; Merleau-Ponty, 1945; Peirce *et al.*, 1998; Varela *et al.*, 1991; Lakoff and Johnson, 1999; Petitot *et al.*, 2000].

survival – because these capacities helped us addressing crucial needs (accomplishing certain goals or avoiding threats) arising from *specific* situations in *specific* environments. As argued by developmental psychologists, human communication presumably emerged from the general ability to participate with others in *collaborative activities* with shared goals and intentions. Humans communicate to request help, inform others of things helpfully, and share attitudes as a way of bonding within the cultural group [Tomasello *et al.*, 2005]. In order to do so, the participants in a given interaction must be able to (1) establish a *common ground*, and (2) view each other as goal-directed, intentional agents with whom they can share emotions, experience and activities. Such kind of communication therefore directly depends on being fully aware and attentive to what's going on in the environment and in the mind of the other participants.

intentionality

common ground

The centrality of context is also striking from the point of view of early language acquisition. Children develop based on their sensorimotor experiences with the physical environment, and this naturally also holds for the acquisition of their native language, starting at about 10 months. Learning always takes place in environments in which the child can get sensory information and perform actions to interact with other people. And indeed, among the first words learned by children, we notice that a large portion are directly grounded in the physical senses [Bailey *et al.*, 1997; Caselli *et al.*, 2000].

language acquisition

2.2.2 Situated human language processing

But what is exactly the *nature* of this connection between human language processing and the situated context? The hypothesis that we put forward in this thesis is that the connection should take the form of a close *bi-directional coupling* between dialogue processing and the various processes involved in building up and maintaining situation awareness. These cognitive activities are inextricably linked. Their interdependence is expressed by a constant exchange of information. Our awareness of the situations affects how we understand dialogue and, through dialogue, we can also further our understanding of those situations. [Kruijff *et al.*, 2009].

Figure 2.1: Mounted helmet for eye-tracking experiments.

bi-directional coupling

Furthermore, several experimental studies in psycholinguistics and neurosciences have demonstrated that the connection between language comprehension and the situated context (and more specifically the visual scene) is also closely *time-locked*, and already present at the phoneme or sub-word level. This has been demonstrated by analyses of saccadic eye movements in visual scenes – based on the idea that eye movements can serve as indications of underlying cognitive processes [Tanenhaus et al., 1995; Allopenna et al., 1998; Knoeferle and Crocker, 2006] – and by neuroscience-based studies of event-related brain potentials [Van Berkum, 2004].

These findings have important implications on how we view language comprehension. Upon hearing a spoken utterance, humans do not wait for the end of the utterance to start processing it. As soon as they have recognised a given morpheme, they start building partial syntactic and semantic interpretations – and they relate these to the situated context.

<small>incrementality</small>
Language comprehension must therefore be seen as being essentially an *incremental*, "word-by-word" process [Crocker, 1999]. At each incremental step, situation awareness plays a double role:

- as a *disambiguation* tool on the existing representations, by pruning the unlikely or incoherent interpretations;

- and as an *anticipatory* tool, raising expectations about what is likely to appear next [Altmann and Steedman, 1988; Van Berkum et al., 2005].

<small>parallelism</small>
Moreover, the existence of such close interaction between cognitive processes also illustrates another defining characteristic of human language processing (and of human cognition in general, for that matter): its high degree of *parallelism*. When we try to comprehend an utterance, all levels of analysis – acoustic, morpho-syntactical, semantic, pragmatic – are activated in parallel and mutually constrain each other to guide the processing.

2.2.3 Five working hypotheses

We have now laid out the basic theoretical "tenets" of our perspective on human language processing and situated context. Let's briefly recapitulate some of the essential facts what we have learned in this section:

<small>situation awareness</small>
1. **Situation awareness** is crucial to spoken dialogue comprehension and production.

<small>pragmatics</small>
2. **Pragmatics** should be taken seriously, and **context** put at the very centre of processing.

3. Linguistic and non-linguistic processes *cannot be isolated* from each other. They are are strongly interdependent, and must be seen as

"**permeable glass boxes**" which can exchange information *while* processing to help guide the interpretation process (i.e. gradual refinement of internal representations, selective attention).

4. Spoken utterances are processed in an **incremental** fashion, and context is exploited all along the way, either to **disambiguate** existing representations, or to **anticipate** future ones.

5. All levels of analysis, linguistic and non-linguistic, should occur in **parallel** and complement each others internal representations.

These five points constitute five basic *"working hypotheses"* for our approach. As will be explained in the next chapters, many of our design choices and implementation strategies – such as the use of particular linguistic formalisms (Chapter 3), the software architecture in which our system is integrated (Chapter 4), or the type of features that we use to discriminate the possible interpretations of an utterance (Chapter 6) – are all direct applications of these insights.

2.3 Summary of the chapter

Here is a short summary of what we learned in this chapter:

- We described the various *linguistic phenomena* encountered in spoken dialogue, such as the presence of filled pauses, repetitions, corrections, speech overlaps, back-channels, speech repairs, sentence fragments, or slightly agrammatical utterances. We also provided a theoretical analysis for the syntactic treatment of disfluencies, which will serve as a basis for the grammar relaxation mechanism presented in Chapter 6.

- In the second part of this chapter, we explained the fundamental characteristics of *situated human language processing*, based on experimental studies in psycholinguistics and cognitive science. We concluded by summing up these characteristics in five "working hypotheses", which – as we will see in the next chapters – will constitute the backbone of our approach to spoken dialogue comprehension.

3

Theoretical foundations

This chapter lays out the theoretical foundations of our work. We detail the formalisms used at the *syntactic*, *semantic* and *pragmatic* levels of our architecture. We first describe the grammatical formalism used for syntactic parsing, which is *Combinatory Categorial Grammar*. We then present the logic used to express the semantic representations, called *Hybrid Logic Dependency Semantics*, and discuss its main formal properties. We also describe how the mapping between syntactic and semantic structures is practically realised. Finally, we explain how the discourse and event structures are represented.

3.1 Combinatory Categorial Grammar

Categorial Grammar (CG) is one of the oldest family of grammatical formalisms developed in modern linguistics (along with dependency grammars, with whom they share many common insights). CG was first proposed by Adjukiewicz [1935] and subsequently modified by Bar-Hillel [1953]; Lambek [1958]; Dowty [1979]; Ades and Steedman [1982]; Steedman [1989], inter alia.

All forms of categorial grammars share a strong commitment to the *principle of compositionality* [Frege, 1892; Montague, 1974] – that is, the assumption that the meaning of a complex expression is determined by its *structure* and the *meanings of its constituents*. Or to put it slightly differently, the assumption that syntax and semantics are *homomorphically related* and may be derived in tandem.

All modern flavours of CG are *fully lexicalised* grammar formalisms. That is, all the language-specific information is contained in the *lexicon*, not in grammar rules, as in classical context-free grammars. The responsibility of defining the syntactic forms is done at the level of individual lexical items. The syntactic behaviour of each morpheme (in terms of subcategorisation

Categorial
Grammar

frame, possible features and constraints, multi-word combinations, etc.) can therefore be specified with great precision, leading to a much more fine-grained level of grammatical description.

Combinatory Categorial Grammar

One of the most recent (and most successful) formulation of CG is **Combinatory Categorial Grammar** [Steedman, 2000]. It combines the advantages of being both *linguistically very expressive* and *efficiently parsable*. It has been used to model a wide range of linguistic phenomena [Steedman, 2000; Steedman and Baldridge, 2009], most notably a unified – and very elegant – treatment of extraction and coordination.

As Tree Adjoining Grammar, CCG is a *mildly context-sensitive* formalism, and is therefore able to account for non-context-free linguistic phenomena such as Germanic crossing dependencies. Another remarkable trait of CCG is its *flexible constituent structure*, which is of particular interest for our purpose since it allows the construction of *incremental derivations*. It is also a formalism which is perfectly suited for *island parsing* [Carroll, 1983], a mechanism devised to extract *partial analyses* out of a given utterance.

Finally, CCG has a completely *transparent interface* between surface syntax and the underlying semantic representation, including predicate-argument structure, quantification and information structure.

For all these reasons – linguistic expressivity, efficiency, flexible constituent structure, possibility for partial analyses, and transparent syntax-semantics interface – CCG is a grammatical formalism which is particularly well suited to the specific needs of our dialogue comprehension system.

3.1.1 Lexicon

lexicon

The core of a CCG grammar is a *lexicon*. Each entry in the lexicon is a pair consisting of a word and an associated category, which contains both syntactic and semantic information:

$$\text{red} \vdash \text{adj} : @_{d:\text{-color}} \ (\ \textbf{red}\ ) \tag{3.1}$$

The lexical entry in (3.1) defines the word 'red' as being of syntactic category **adj**, and binds it to a particular semantic representation, which we write $@_{d:\text{-color}}$ (**red**) (more on this in the next section).

The category **adj** is an atomic category, which does not take any argument. We can also define complex categories, using the *slash notation*. A category X/Y denotes a lexical item which, if given an argument of type Y to its right, will return a result of type X. For instance, a determiner such as 'the' can be assigned the category **np/n**, meaning that if it is associated to a common noun of type **n**, the determiner will produce a noun phrase **np**.

Likewise, the category $X\backslash Y$ denotes a lexical item which, if given an argument of type Y to its left, will return a result of type X.

3.1.2 Combinatory rules

CCG makes use of a set of *combinatory rules* which are used to assemble categories to form larger pieces of syntactic and semantic structure. The most simple ones, which are used in all flavours of categorial grammars, are the forward and backward applications:

combinatory rules

$$X/Y \quad Y \Rightarrow X \qquad (>)$$
$$Y \quad X\backslash Y \Rightarrow X \qquad (<)$$

The first rule states that we can form a larger constituent of type X by assembling a constituent of type X/Y and a constituent of type Y which is to its right. The second rule embodies the same principle, but in the left direction.

CCG also allows for more sophisticated combinatory rules, such as forward/backward composition (**B**) and type-raising (**T**):

$$X/Y \quad Y/Z \Rightarrow X/Z \qquad (>\mathbf{B})$$
$$Y\backslash Z \quad X\backslash Y \Rightarrow X\backslash Z \qquad (<\mathbf{B})$$

$$X \Rightarrow Y/(Y\backslash X) \qquad (>\mathbf{T})$$
$$X \Rightarrow Y\backslash(Y/X) \qquad (<\mathbf{T})$$

The simultaneous build of the syntactic and semantic structures is done using these combinatory rules. The applicability of these rules can moreover be controlled through *modalised slashes* [Baldridge and Kruijff, 2003].

3.1.3 Derivations

Given a lexicon and a set of combinatory rules, parsing a given utterance is achieved in polynomial time. The syntactic structure can then be extracted by looking at the derivational history of a parse. Figure 3.1 offers an illustrative example (du stands for "discourse unit").

As a final note, it should be noted that CCG derivations are *monotonic* – there are no movements or traces in Categorial Grammar, contrary to transformational approaches of natural language syntax (e.g. Chomsky [1957] and following).

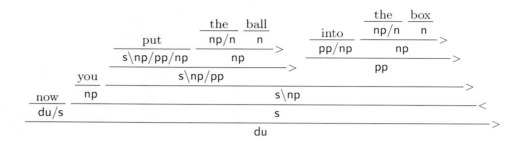

Figure 3.1: CCG parse for the utterance "now you put the ball into the box".

3.2 Hybrid Logic Dependency Semantics

In this section[1], we present the logical formalism which we use to express the *semantic representations* of our dialogue system. The formalism is called **Hybrid Logic Dependency Semantics** [Baldridge and Kruijff, 2002]. It provides an explicit encoding for a wide range of semantic information, including dependency relations between heads and dependents [Tesnière, 1959; Sgall *et al.*, 1986; Mel'čuk, 1988], tense and aspect [Moens and Steedman, 1988], spatio-temporal structure, contextual reference, and information structure [Kruijff, 2001].

What we mean here by "semantic representation" is more precisely the *linguistically realised* meaning. Contrary to most formalisms derived from Fregean semantics (notably DRT), we only represent the meaning as it is realised in the utterance, without trying to evaluate the *state of the world* denoted by it.

Hybrid Logic Dependency Semantics [HLDS] is based on *hybrid modal logic*. We start with some (brief) generalities about hybrid logics, and then proceed to describe the HLDS formalism itself.

3.2.1 Hybrid logic

Relational structures are a fundamental modeling tool in science. It is ubiquitous in artificial intelligence, computer science, linguistics and mathematics. *Modal logic* provides an efficient and logically sound way of talking about such structures [Blackburn *et al.*, 2001].

---

[1] Most of the content of this section is derived from [Baldridge and Kruijff, 2002; Kruijff, 2001; Blackburn, 2000; Areces and Blackburn, 2001].

Classical modal logic however suffers from – as Carlos Aceres puts it –
a surprising *"asymmetry"*. Although the concept of states ("worlds") are
at the heart of model theory (cf. the definition of Kripke models), there
is no way to directly *reference* specific states in the object language. This
asymmetry is at the root of several theoretical and practical problems facing
modal logic [Blackburn, 2000; Areces and Blackburn, 2001].

Hybrid logic provides an elegant solution to many of these problems. It
extends standard modal logic while retaining decidability and favorable complexity [Areces *et al.*, 2001; Areces and Blackburn, 2001]. The strategy is to
add *nominals*, a new sort of basic formula with which we can explicitly name
states *in the object language*. Next to propositions, nominals are therefore
first-class citizens in the object language.

Hybrid logic

nominals

Each nominal names a unique state. To get to that state, we add a new
operator, called the *satisfaction operator*, that enables us to "jump" to the
state named by the nominal. The satisfaction operator is written $@_i$, where
i is a nominal.

satisfaction
operator

Formal definitions

We first present in **Definition 1** the formal specification of the object language for the basic hybrid multimodal language $\mathcal{H}(@)$. **Definitions 2** and
3 then provide the *model-theoretical interpretation* of such hybrid language,
based on Kripke models.

Definition 1 *(**Basic hybrid multimodal language** $\mathcal{H}(@)$)*. *We start
with a set of propositional symbols $PROP = \{p, q, p', q', ...\}$, a set of modality
labels $MOD = \{\pi, \pi', ...\}$, and a nonempty set $NOM = \{i, j, ...\}$ disjoint
from PROP and MOD. We define the well-formed formulas of the basic
hybrid multimodal language $\mathcal{H}(@)$ over PROP, MOD and NOM as such:*

$$WFF := i \mid p \mid \neg\phi \mid \phi \wedge \psi \mid \phi \vee \psi \mid \phi \rightarrow \psi \mid \langle\pi\rangle\phi \mid [\pi]\phi \mid @_i\phi \quad (3.2)$$

A formula $@_i\phi$ states that the formula ϕ holds at the (unique) state named
by i. Or to put it in more operational terms, the formula $@_i\phi$ could be
translated in the following way: "go to the (unique!) state named by i, and
check whether ϕ is true at that state".

Definition 2 *(**Kripke models**)*. *Such a language is interpreted on models (often called Kripke models). A model $\mathcal{M}$ is a triple $(W, \{R_\pi \mid \pi \in MOD\}, V)$. W is a non-empty set (its elements are called* states *or* nodes*),* and each R_π is a binary relation on W. The pair $(W, \{R_\pi \mid \pi \in MOD\})$ is called the **frame** *underlying* $\mathcal{M}$, and $\mathcal{M}$ is said to be a model based on this frame. The function V is called the hybrid valuation. It is a function with domain $PROP \cup NOM$ and range $Pow(W)$; it tells us at which states (if any) each propositional symbol is true. We additionally require that for each nominal i, the valuation $V(i)$ be a singleton subset of W. We call the unique state in $V(i)$ the *denotation of* i.

Definition 3 (*Satisfaction and validity*). *Interpretation on models is carried out using the Kripke satisfaction definition. Let* $\mathcal{M} = (W, \{R_\pi \mid \pi \in MOD\}, V)$ *and* $w \in W$. *Then:*

$$
\begin{array}{lll}
\mathcal{M}, w \models p & \text{iff} & w \in V(p), \text{ where } p \in PROP \\
\mathcal{M}, w \models i & \text{iff} & w \in V(i), \text{ where } i \in NOM \\
\mathcal{M}, w \models \neg\phi & \text{iff} & \mathcal{M}, w \not\models \phi \\
\mathcal{M}, w \models \phi \wedge \psi & \text{iff} & \mathcal{M}, w \models \phi \text{ and } \mathcal{M}, w \models \psi \\
\mathcal{M}, w \models \phi \vee \psi & \text{iff} & \mathcal{M}, w \models \phi \text{ or } \mathcal{M}, w \models \psi \\
\mathcal{M}, w \models \phi \to \psi & \text{iff} & \mathcal{M}, w \not\models \phi \text{ or } \mathcal{M}, w \models \psi \\
\mathcal{M}, w \models \langle\pi\rangle\phi & \text{iff} & \exists w'(wR_\pi w' \ \& \ \mathcal{M}, w' \models \phi) \\
\mathcal{M}, w \models [\pi]\phi & \text{iff} & \forall w'(wR_\pi w' \Rightarrow \mathcal{M}, w' \models \phi) \\
\mathcal{M}, w \models @_i\phi & \text{iff} & \mathcal{M}, w' \models \phi, \text{ where } w' \text{ is the denotation of } i.
\end{array}
$$

If $\mathcal{M}, w \models \phi$, we say that the formula ϕ is satisfied in $\mathcal{M}$ at the state w.

A practical example

Let us consider a practical example to illustrate how hybrid logic can be applied to represent relational structures. (3.3) is an attribute-value matrix [AVM], a widely used relational structure in computational linguistics.

$$
\begin{bmatrix} \text{SUBJ} & \boxed{1} \begin{bmatrix} \text{AGR} & foo \\ \text{PRED} & bar \end{bmatrix} \\ \text{COMP} & \begin{bmatrix} \text{SUBJ} & \boxed{1} \end{bmatrix} \end{bmatrix} \tag{3.3}
$$

Such structure can be efficiently expressed with a hybrid logic formula, as (3.4) shows. Figure 3.2 gives a graphical illustration of the same formula. The nodes denote individual states, and the edges are modalities. The fact that states can be explicitly referenced in the object language is what allows us to represent the reentrancy mechanism of the AVM.

$$
\begin{array}{l} @(\langle\text{SUBJ}\rangle(i \wedge \langle\text{AGR}\rangle\mathbf{foo} \wedge \langle\text{PRED}\rangle\mathbf{bar}) \wedge \\ \quad \langle\text{COMP}\rangle\langle\text{SUBJ}\rangle i) \end{array} \tag{3.4}
$$

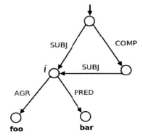

Figure 3.2: Graphical representation of the hybrid formula 3.4.

Sorting strategy

Another interesting characteristic of hybrid logics is the possibility to *sort* atomic symbols. Sorting is a strategy that has been proposed by various authors to create ontologically rich representations of meaning [Vendler, 1967; Dowty, 1979; van Benthem, 1997].

Different sorts of nominals can be introduced in the object language to build up a rich sortal ontology. This make it possible to capture the rich ontologies of lexical databases like WordNet in a clear and concise fashion, while retaining decidability and a favorable complexity [Baldridge and Kruijff, 2002; Areces and ten Cate, 2006].

3.2.2 Encoding linguistic meaning

Using hybrid logic, we are able to capture three essential aspects of linguistic meaning:

1. *structural complexity* (due to the use of modal logic to represent linguistic meaning via sophisticated relational structures)

2. *ontological richness* (due to the sorting strategy);

3. the possibility to *refer* (due to the introduction of nominals in the object language).

We can represent an expression's linguistically realized meaning as a conjunction of modalized terms, anchored by the nominal that identifies the head's proposition:

$$@_{h:\, \text{sort}_h}(\mathbf{prop}_h \wedge \langle \delta_i \rangle (\mathrm{d}_i : \text{sort}_{d_i} \wedge \mathbf{dep}_i)) \qquad (3.5)$$

In (3.5), the head proposition nominal is labeled by h. $\mathbf{prop}_h$ represents the *elementary predication* of the nominal h. The dependency relations (such as AGENT, PATIENT, RESULT, etc.) are modeled as *modal relations* $\langle \delta_i \rangle$. Each dependent is labeled by a specific *nominal*, here d_i. Features attached to a nominal (e.g. $\langle \text{NUM} \rangle$, $\langle \text{QUANTIFICATION} \rangle$, etc.) are specified in the same way.

Figure 3.3 gives an example of logical form, written in HLDS.

$$@_{w_0:cognition}(\mathbf{want} \wedge$$
$$<\text{MOOD}> \text{ind} \wedge$$
$$<\text{TENSE}> \text{pres} \wedge$$
$$<\text{ACTOR}>(i_0 : person \wedge \mathbf{I} \wedge$$
$$<\text{NUMBER}> \text{sg}) \wedge$$
$$<\text{ECOMP}>(t_0 : action\text{-}motion \wedge \mathbf{take} \wedge$$
$$<\text{ACTOR}> y_0 : person \wedge$$
$$<\text{PATIENT}>(m_0 : thing \wedge \mathbf{mug} \wedge$$
$$<\text{DELIMITATION}> \text{unique} \wedge$$
$$<\text{NUMBER}> \text{sg} \wedge$$
$$<\text{QUANTIFICATION}> \text{specific\_singular})) \wedge$$
$$<\text{PATIENT}>(y_0 : person \wedge \mathbf{you} \wedge$$
$$<\text{NUMBER}> \text{sg}))$$

Figure 3.3: HLDS semantics for the utterance 'I want you to take the mug'.

3.3 Syntax-semantics interface

How do we derive a semantic representation from a particular syntactic structure? In our CCG grammar, this is realized by augmenting the syntactic rules with semantic information. Since CCG is a lexicalist theory, this information is specified directly in the lexicon. The formal properties of the syntax-semantics interface are not detailed here, the interested reader is invited to consult Baldridge and Kruijff [2002] for more information[2].

We illustrate below two concrete examples of CCG derivation, along with the associated HLDS semantics.

Example 1

The parsed utterance is "The ball is red".

---

[2] See also White [2006] for a translation from HLDS forms to DRT.

- **Lexicon**

  the ⊢   np : a / n : b (3.6)

  with a being defined as $@_a \begin{pmatrix} p \wedge \\ \langle \text{NUM} \rangle \text{ sg} \wedge \\ \langle \text{DELIM} \rangle \text{ unique} \wedge \\ \langle \text{QUANT} \rangle \text{ specific} \end{pmatrix}$

  and b as $@_b p$

  ball ⊢   n : $@_{b:\text{thing}}$ (**ball**)   (3.7)

  is ⊢   s : c \ np : r / adj : s (3.8)

  with c being defined as $@_{c:\text{ascription}} \begin{pmatrix} \textbf{be} \wedge \\ \langle \text{MOOD} \rangle \text{ind} \wedge \\ \langle \text{TENSE} \rangle \text{pres} \wedge \\ \langle \text{SUBJ} \rangle (r \wedge p) \wedge \\ \langle \text{RESTR} \rangle r \wedge \\ \langle \text{SCOPE} \rangle (s \wedge q) \end{pmatrix}$

  and r as $@_r p$
  and s as $@_s q$

  red ⊢   adj : $@_{d:\text{-color}}$ (**red**)   (3.9)

- **Syntactic derivation**

  With the lexical information we provided, we can derive the semantic representation for the utterance "the ball is red" in just three steps (to save space, we don't show the entire premises, and instead redirect to the equation numbers).

$$\frac{\text{np/n} : (3.6) \quad \text{n} : (3.7)}{\text{np} : @_{b:\text{thing}} \begin{pmatrix} \textbf{ball} \wedge \\ \langle \text{NUM} \rangle \text{ sg} \wedge \\ \langle \text{DELIM} \rangle \text{ unique} \wedge \\ \langle \text{QUANT} \rangle \text{ specific} \end{pmatrix}} > \quad (3.10)$$

$$\frac{\text{s\textbackslash np/adj} : (3.8) \quad \text{adj} : (3.9)}{\text{s} : @_{c:\text{ascription}} \begin{pmatrix} \textbf{be} \wedge \\ \langle \text{MOOD} \rangle \text{ind} \wedge \\ \langle \text{TENSE} \rangle \text{pres} \wedge \\ \langle \text{SUBJ} \rangle (r \wedge p) \wedge \\ \langle \text{RESTR} \rangle r \wedge \\ \langle \text{SCOPE} \rangle (\text{s:q-color} \wedge \textbf{red}) \end{pmatrix} \backslash \text{np} : @_r p} > \quad (3.11)$$

$$s : @_{c:\text{ascription}} \begin{pmatrix} \mathbf{be} \wedge \\ \langle \text{MOOD} \rangle \text{ind} \wedge \\ \langle \text{TENSE} \rangle \text{pres} \wedge \\ \langle \text{SUBJ} \rangle \begin{pmatrix} \text{b:thing} \wedge \mathbf{ball} \wedge \\ \langle \text{NUM} \rangle \text{ sg} \wedge \\ \langle \text{DELIM} \rangle \text{ unique} \\ \langle \text{QUANT} \rangle \text{ specific} \end{pmatrix} \wedge \\ \langle \text{RESTR} \rangle \text{b} \wedge \\ \langle \text{SCOPE} \rangle (\text{s:q-color} \wedge \mathbf{red}) \end{pmatrix} \overset{\text{np}:(3.10) \quad \text{s\textbackslash np}:(3.11)}{<} \quad (3.12)$$

Example 2

Figure 3.4 presents a complete syntactic analysis for the utterance "robot I want the red ball where is it". Due to space constraints, only the main syntactic categories are shown. The features and the semantic representation associated to each intermediate category are omitted. Note that the final syntactic category is not a sentence, but a *discourse unit*, labeled du.

3.4 Segmented Discourse Representation Theory

Once a semantic interpretation for a given utterance has been built, it must be integrated into a larger *discourse structure*. How do we represent this discourse structure? Our dialogue system is based on **Segmented Discourse Representation Theory** (SDRT) [Asher and Lascarides, 2003; Lascarides and Asher, 2007].

Segmented Discourse Representation Theory

SDRT is a formal approach to discourse interpretation which is grounded in *dynamic semantics* (notably DRT, cf. Kamp and Reyle [1993]), and extended with *rhetorical relations*.

3.4.1 Dynamic semantics

dynamic semantics

In traditional formal semantics [Montague, 1988], the content of a discourse is defined as the *set of models* ("'possible worlds'") that it satisfies. They are therefore typically unable to model how the interpretation of the current sentence is dependent on the interpretations of those that precede it [Lascarides and Asher, 2007]. As a consequence, traditional formal semantics is inadequate to model most intersentential phenomena, like temporal and

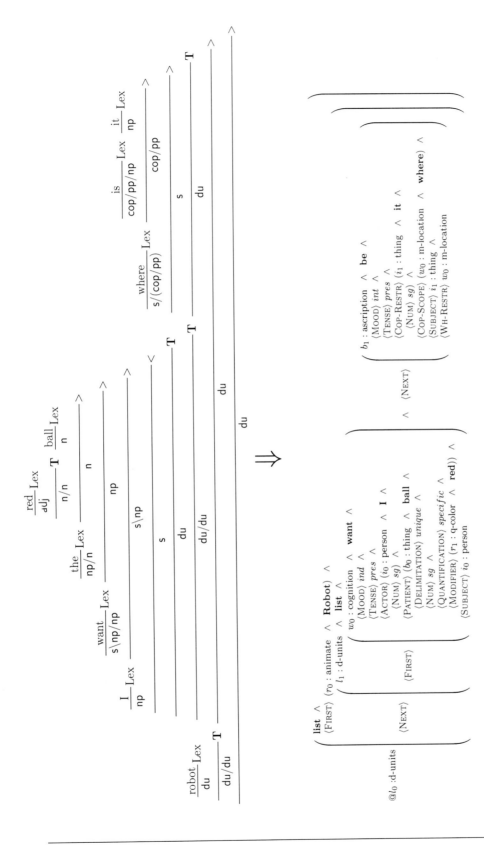

Figure 3.4: Example of syntactic analysis using Combinatory Categorial Grammar. Above, the derivation history for the utterance "robot I want the red ball where is it". Due to space constraints, only the main syntactic categories are shown. Below, we present the semantic representation extracted at the end of the parse, expressed in HLDS.

pronominal anaphora. For instance, in (3.13-3.14), how do we express the fact that the man who ordered a beer is the same as the one who walked in?

> The man walked in. (3.13)
> He ordered a beer. (3.14)

Context Change Potential

Dynamic semantics, on the other hand, views the meaning of a given discourse as a *relation* (or more precisely, a *function*) between contexts. This function is called *Context Change Potential*. Contrary to Montagovian semantics, dynamic semantics is also generally *non-compositional* – i.e. you cannot define the meaning of a discourse as a simple, static composition of its parts. Indeed, in addition to contributing to the "static" content of a discourse, expressions like indefinite NPs make a *dynamic* contribution to it by introducing new referents.

Discourse Representation Theory

The most well-known theory based on dynamic semantics is **Discourse Representation Theory** [Kamp and Reyle, 1993].

3.4.2 Rhetorical relations

Dynamic semantics theories typically explore a relatively restricted set of pragmatic phenomena, mainly focusing on the effects of logical structure on anaphora. They typically fail to take into account the *discourse structure* (i.e. rhetorical relations between discourse segments) in their analysis. And as evidenced by researchers in discourse analysis, *understanding discourse structure* is absolutely crucial for discourse interpretation [Mann and Thompson, 1986; Mann *et al.*, 1992].

rhetorical relations

Asher and Lascarides [2003] provide two interesting examples to motivate the use of *rhetorical relations* in modeling discourse structure.

Example 1: pronoun resolution

Consider this simple discourse:

> John had a great evening last night. (3.15)
> He had a great meal. (3.16)
> He ate salmon. (3.17)
> He devoured lots of cheese. (3.18)
> He won a dancing competition. (3.19)
> ??It was a beautiful pink. (3.20)

In DRT, nothing would prevent the pronoun 'it' in (3.20) to pick the salmon as the referent. The theory clearly overgenerates the possible interpretations. We need some notion of rhetorical structure to be able to specify more precisely the possible antecedents for the pronoun.

SDRT solves the problem by introducing a set of rhetorical relations between the segments, as illustrated in Figure 3.5. SDRT can then easily rule out the salmon as an antecedent for 'it' by using a right-frontier constraint (cf. Asher and Lascarides [2003]).

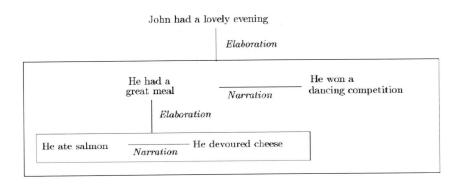

Figure 3.5: Discourse structure of (3.15)-(3.20).

Example 2: temporal structure

Consider these two examples:

$$\text{John fell. Mary helped him up.} \quad (3.21)$$
$$\text{John fell. Mary pushed him.} \quad (3.22)$$

In (3.21), the textual order reflects the temporal one, whereas (3.22) does not. The compositional semantics of both examples are insufficient for distinguishing their interpretations, as they have the same temporal and aspectual classes. The additional bit of information we need resides in rhetorical relations, which will be *Narration* for (3.21) and *Explanation* for (3.22).

3.4.3 The SDRT approach in brief

To sum up, SDRT combines two paradigms in discourse interpretation: *dynamic semantics* and *discourse analysis*. The theory attempts to explicit the interactions between the semantic content of the segments and the global, pragmatic structure of the discouse – it can therefore be seen as a model of the *semantics-pragmatics interface*. Note that the basic units are segmented and analysed according to their *propositional content*, and not e.g. on their attentional or intentional content, like in Grosz and Sidner [1986].

For more details regarding the linguistic and formal motivations behind SDRT, the reader is invited to consult Asher and Lascarides [2003].

How do we apply SDRT to the specific needs of our dialogue comprehension system? First, the so-called "*formulas*" of SDRT are expressed in the HLDS formalism we introduced in this chapter. These formulas are connected with each other by rhetorical relations, which (since we are dealing with dialogue) most often take the form of *conversational moves*. In addition to this, *anaphoric relations* are also expressed between discourse referents, anchored by their HLDS nominals.

The SDRT-based discourse structure can be used as a precious resource to define the *linguistic context* of a particular dialogue. This context can then be fruitfully exploited to guide the processing, e.g. by priming the speech recognition (Chapter 5), or by discriminating the possible interpretations of a given utterance (Chapter 6).

3.4.4 Event structure

event structure

Additionally to the usual discourse structure, an *event structure* is used to model temporal and aspectual information. It is based on a temporal ontology structured on notions of causation and consequence rather than on purely temporal primitives.

nucleus

The elementary event-complex is called a *nucleus*. A nucleus is a tripartite structure, consisting of a "*preparation*" (the activity bringing the event about), a "*culmination*" (the goal event), and a "*consequent*" (the state ensuing the event). Natural-language categories like aspects, futurates, adverbials, and when-clauses are able to change the temporal/aspectual category of propositions under the control of such a nucleic knowledge representation structure [Moens and Steedman, 1988].

3.5 Summary of the chapter

In this chapter, we introduced the three linguistic formalisms used at (respectively) the *syntactic*, *semantic*, and *pragmatic* levels of our dialogue comprehension system:

- We first described **Combinatory Categorial Grammar**, a grammatical formalism for natural language syntax. It combines several advantages which makes it particularly well suited to our approach, such as its linguistic expressivity, an efficient parsability (in polynomial time), a flexible constituent structure, the possibility of partial analyses, and a transparent syntax-semantics interface.

  The core of a CCG grammar is a lexicon, which associates both syntactic and semantic information. The derivation of a parse for a given utterance is achieved by applying a set of *combinatory rules* to combine categories and form larger pieces of syntactic and semantic structure.

- We then detailed the logical formalism used to express the semantic representations. This formalism is called **Hybrid Logic Dependency Semantics**, and is based on an extension (an "hybridisation") of modal logic. Besides the usual constructions of modal logic, a new artifact is added to the object language: *nominals*. These nominals allow us to directly point to a particular state. The formalism also provides the possibility to *sort* atomic symbols, and hence create *ontologically rich* representations of meaning.

- Finally, we outlined the central tenets of **Segmented Discourse Representation Theory**, the formalism chosen to express the *discourse structure*. This formalism combines hindsights from *dynamic semantics* (the meaning of a given discourse is viewed as a relation between contexts) and *discourse analysis* (every discourse is structured by a set of rhetorical relations). In our approach, the formulas of the discourse structure are expressed in HLDS, and connected by various *conversational moves*. The *discourse referents* can moreover also be connected with each others in case of anaphoric relations.

4
Software architecture

In this chapter, we describe the software architecture in which our approach to robust dialogue processing has been designed and developed. We start by describing the global architecture for the entire cognitive system, then provides details on the components used in the communication subarchitecture. We define the various internal *representations* which are manipulated and shared across the subarchitecture, as well as the *processes* operating on these representations.

Intelligent behaviour relies a combination of highly complex cognitive capacities. An "intelligent" system must be able to actively perceive the environment it finds itself in, reason about it, and achieve goals through plans and actions. As a result, artificial cognitive systems which can support such kind of intelligent behaviour must encompass a large number of distributed and cooperating subsystems, such as computer vision (perception, attention), navigation and manipulation skills (motor control), and various deliberative processes (reasoning, learning, planning).

The design of *software architectures* for such cognitive systems is therefore a very demanding enterprise. Not only must these architectures meet very strong structural and performance requirements, but these requirements are often competing with each other.

For instance, quick reactivity and continuous adaptation to the environment are crucial prerequisites for cognitive systems operating in real physical environments. From this perspective, post-sensory processing overhead should be maintained as low as possible, to keep the system reactive. Yet, at the same time, we may also wish to include general capacities for abstract reasoning in the system (e.g. for language comprehension). Such capacities can unfortunately only be achieved with the help of symbolic processes which are usually slow and result in a high processing overhead, at the expense of reactivity. How do we solve this kind of dilemma?

The answer to this question lies in the careful exploration of the *design space* of cognitive architectures, and the investigation of the possible *compromises* and *trade-offs* which are available within it. This way, we can find out which architectural choices are the most adequate for a given scenario [Hawes *et al.*, 2007b, 2009a].

The next section introduces an architectural schema which attempts to address these issues in a coherent fashion: the *Cognitive Systems Architecture Schema* [CAS]. As we will see, CAS allows us to capture many of the "requirements" for cognitive processing outlined in section 2.2.3. It comes with an associated implementation toolkit, *CAST*, on top of which our implementation has been built.

4.1 Global architecture

<small>architectural schema</small>

We start with the notion of *architectural schema*. An architectural schema is described as a "set of constraints that defines a space of possible architectures". Multiple architectural instantiations – that is, fully specified, concrete architectures – can then be created on basis of such schema.

4.1.1 Cognitive Systems Architecture Schema

<small>Cognitive Systems Architecture Schema</small>

The architectural schema used for this thesis is called the **Cognitive Systems Architecture Schema**, or CAS. Its most important characteristics are (quoted from [Hawes *et al.*, 2009a]):

- *Distributed shared memory*: The schema contains subarchitectures each of which has a blackboard (working memory). These subarchitectures are loosely coupled to reduce complex inter-dependencies. Systems can contain subarchitectures for motor control, vision, action, planning, language etc.

- *Parallel refinement of shared representations*: Each subarchitecture contains a number of processing components which run in parallel and that asynchronously read and update shared information via the subarchitecture specific working memory.

- *Limited privileges*: Each of these subarchitecture working memories is only writable by processes within its subarchitecture, and by a small number of privileged global processes (e.g. a global goal manager).

- *Control of information and processing*: Information flow is controlled by goals generated within the architecture at run time, allowing it to deal with new problems and opportunities. This allows the schema to support different approaches to processing (e.g. incremental processing, forward chaining, backward chaining etc.).

- *Knowledge management by ontologies*: The knowledge used within a subarchitecture is defined by a set of ontologies for that subarchitecture. Relationships between the ontologies in different subarchitectures are defined by a set of general ontologies. These ontologies can also be used to define knowledge at an architecture-general level.

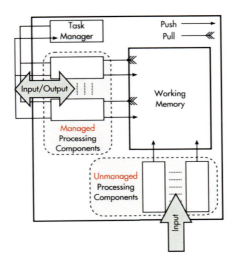

Figure 4.1: A single subarchitecture within the Cognitive Systems Architecture Schema. The subarchitecture includes a set of components, which run in parallel, asynchronously updating shared structures on a common working memory. They can also take input from sensors or give output to actuators. The task manager determines whether managed components are able to run, while unmanaged components always run [Hawes *et al.*, 2009a].

4.1.2 CAST: an implementation toolkit for CAS

CAS comes with an associated implementation toolkit which is called CAST [Hawes *et al.*, 2007a]. CAST allows components written in different languages (mostly Java and C++) to be combined into CAS instantiations, without recompilation or change in components.

CAST is constituted as a distributed collection of subsystems for information processing. Figure 4.2 illustrates the connections between the subarchitectures implemented in our robotic platform. The interested reader is invited to consult [Hawes *et al.*, 2009b; Brenner *et al.*, 2007; Skočaj *et al.*, 2007; Zender *et al.*, 2008; Sjö *et al.*, 2008] for more information on the instantiation of CAST in various robotic scenarios.

As illustrated in Figure 4.1, each subsystem consists of one or more processes, and a working memory. The processes can access sensors, effectors, and the working memory to share information within the subsystem. Processes can be either unmanaged (data-driven) or managed (goal-driven). The execution of the managed processed is directed by the task manager. This enables the subarchitecture to synchronize various forms of information processing.

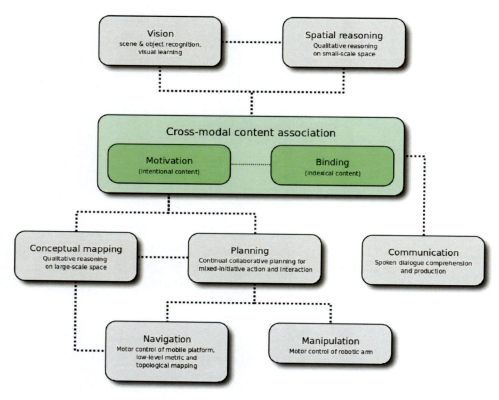

Figure 4.2: Interactions between subarchitectures in CAST

Cross-modal binding

One interesting aspect of CAST we would like to highlight is the way the architecture addresses the *binding problem*. *Binding* is the operation of connecting pieces of information coming from different modalities, but which ultimately refer to the same entity. From the linguistic point of view, this binding functionality is what is used by the communication subsystem to achieve *visual* and *spatial reference resolution*.

binding

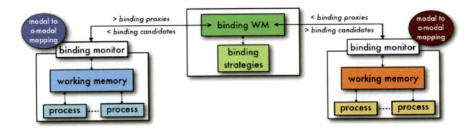

Figure 4.3: Cross-modal interconnectivity

Imagine for instance a visual scene with a blue mug at the centre of a table, which gets mentioned in the course of a dialogue ("hey robot look - this is a blue mug"). The visual modality perceives the blue mug as an object in the scene, whereas the "linguistic modality" (i.e. the dialogue comprehension) perceives a discourse referent named 'blue mug'. The question is how we can connect, or bind, these two pieces of information. Or to put it differently, how we can *ground* the dialogue in the situated environment.

grounding

The basic idea is illustrated in Figure 4.3. Each subsystem can have a *binding monitor* as one of its managed processes. A *binding monitor* is a process which monitors the subsystem's internal working memory. As soon as the working memory contains content that could be connected to content in other modalities, the binding monitor translates this content using a mapping between the subsystem's own representations, and an *amodal* format used in a particular subarchitecture called the *binder*. This is based on the idea of ontology-mediated *information fusion* [Kruijff et al., 2006].

binding monitor

information fusion

The resulting representation is then written from the working memory into the binder. There it acts as a *proxy* for content in the originating subsystem. The binder now applies strategies to combine proxies with similar content, but coming from different subsystems. Proxies that can be combined to form unions. The power of the binding mechanism is its flexibility: we can use a mixture of early- and late-fusion, and represent content at any level of abstraction [Kruijff et al., 2007; Jacobsson et al., 2007].

proxy

The "binder" subarchitecture provides us with a (mediated) access to the *situated context*. At each stage of processing, the various processing components involved in dialogue comprehension can query the binder in order to know which objects are currently in the visual scene. This allows us to perform *context-sensitive* language processing – a core aspect of our approach. Chapters 5 and 6 will explain how this information is then applied to *anticipate* or *discriminate* the spoken inputs.

The design of CAS and CAST also provides interesting solutions to many other architectural problems (pertaining e.g. to information filtering, processing management, action fusion, etc.), which, due to space constraints, we don't have the time to discuss in this thesis. For details, see [Jacobsson *et al.*, 2007; Hawes *et al.*, 2007a,b, 2009a].

4.2 The communication subarchitecture

Let us now concentrate on the subarchitecture which is most relevant for the topic of this thesis: the *communication subarchitecture*. Figure 4.4 illustrates the information flow in the subarchitecture for spoken dialogue comprehension (dialogue production components are omitted). All the structures and components described in the next pages are comprised in this schema.

We start by defining the various internal *representations* which are manipulated and shared across the subarchitecture, and then proceed with a description of the different *processes* which operate on these representations.

4.2.1 Representations

We describe below four important representations used through the communication subarchitecture: the *word lattice* (which is generated by the speech recogniser), the *logical form* (the semantic representation build by the incremental parser), the *packed logical form* (a "compressed" set of logical forms), and the *discourse structure* (representing, well, the discourse structure).

Word lattices

word lattices

The speech recogniser outputs partial recognition hypotheses in the form of *word lattices*. Each recognition hypothesis corresponds to a possible path in the word lattice. These paths are *weighted* paths, some hypotheses being more likely than others.

The weights are computed on basis of two numerical scores provided by the ASR: an *acoustic score* (based on the acoustic model) and a *semantic*

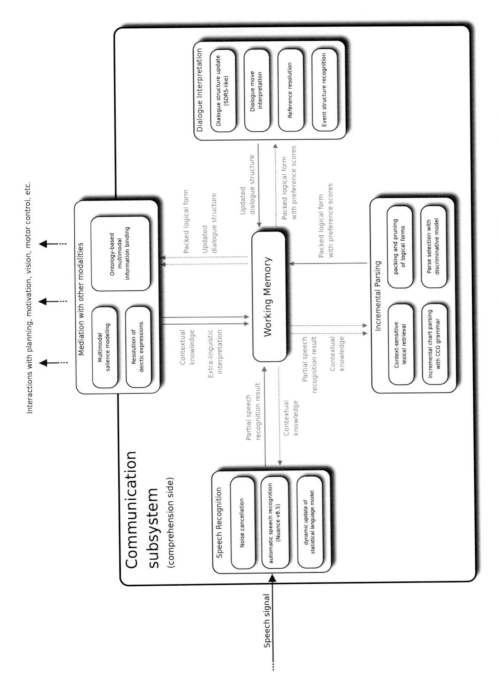

Figure 4.4: Schematic view of the architecture for spoken dialogue comprehension.

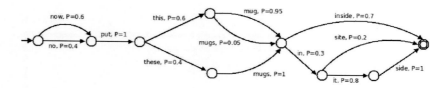

Figure 4.5: Recognition lattice for the utterance "now put this mug inside".

score (based on a semantic model incorporated in the ASR).

Logical forms

Hybrid Logic Dependency Semantics

The semantic representations are expressed via *logical forms*. These logical forms are formally defined using a *hybrid logic* framework named **Hybrid Logic Dependency Semantics** [HLDS], that we already reviewed in some detail in section 3.2. HLDS expresses linguistically realised meaning as *ontologically richly sorted, relational structures*. These relational structures are defined as conjunctions of modalised terms, anchored by the nominal that identifies the head's proposition.

On the implementation level, logical forms are practically defined as sets of nominals, along with a reference to the root node. A logical form is therefore a tuple $\{Noms, root\}$, where:

1. *Noms* is a set of nominals. Each nominal includes an identifier, an ontological sort, a (possibly empty) logical proposition, a (possibly empty) list of features and a (possibly empty) list of dependency relations.

2. *root* is a reference to the root nominal.

The logical form representation defined above is a model of HLDS formulas which is convenient for computational purposes. The "conjunction of modalised terms" is simply expressed as a list of features and a list of dependency relations, and the nominal anchoring the head's proposition is simply assigned to the *root* nominal. Figure 4.6 gives an example of logical form, which we have already seen in the previous chapter. Figure 4.7 shows a graphical illustration of the same logical form (the nominals being shown as nodes, and the modalities as dependency edges).

$@_{w_0:cognition}(\textbf{want} \wedge$
        $<\textsc{Mood}>$ ind $\wedge$
        $<\textsc{Tense}>$ pres $\wedge$
        $<\textsc{Actor}>(i_0 : person \wedge \textbf{I} \wedge$
                $<\textsc{Number}>$ sg) $\wedge$
        $<\textsc{EComp}>(t_0 : action\text{-}motion \wedge \textbf{take} \wedge$
                $<\textsc{Actor}>y_0 : person \wedge$
                $<\textsc{Patient}>(m_0 : thing \wedge \textbf{mug} \wedge$
                        $<\textsc{Delimitation}>$ unique $\wedge$
                        $<\textsc{Number}>$ sg $\wedge$
                        $<\textsc{Quantification}>$ specific_singular)) $\wedge$
        $<\textsc{Patient}>(y_0 : person \wedge \textbf{you} \wedge$
                $<\textsc{Number}>$ sg))

Figure 4.6: Logical form for the utterance 'I want you to take the mug'

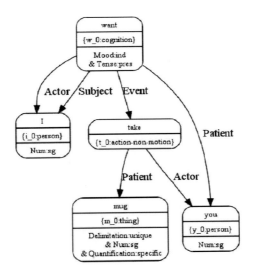

Figure 4.7: Graphical representation of the logical form expressed in 4.6 (automatically generated by the parser, based on the DOT library).

Packed logical forms

The syntactic analysis of most utterances is likely to yield a large number of possible logical forms. This is due to three main reasons:

- Recall that the comprehension system is not parsing single word strings, but complete *word lattices*. A word lattice encompasses several alternative recognition hypotheses in a single structure. The result of parsing such structure will therefore comprise, for each recognition hypothesis, the set of its possible interpretations.

- As we already mentioned in the introduction, our approach to robust parsing of spoken inputs relies on *grammar relaxation* techniques. Relaxing the set of grammatical constraints has for logical consequence an increase in the number of possible parses.

- Finally, we should not forget that language in itself is *inherently ambiguous*, and the comprehension system must deal with various kinds of lexical, syntactic, semantic or pragmatic ambiguities.

The problem we are facing here is that maintaining hundreds of distinct logical forms in parallel in the system is likely to result in a high processing overhead. To address this issue, we devised an algorithm which could "pack" all the alternative interpretations in a single representation, similar to the packing algorithms developed for HPSG [Oepen and Carroll, 2000; Carroll and Oepen, 2005]. We call this representation a *packed logical form*. A packed logical form [PLF] represents content similar across the different analyses of a given input as a single graph, using over- and underspecification of how different nodes can be connected to capture lexical and syntactic forms of ambiguity.

Figure 4.8 gives an example of such packed logical form. PLFs are construed with two basic elements: *packing nodes* and *packing edges*. A packing node groups a set of nominals sharing identical properties under a particular subset of the logical forms. The packing edges are then used to connect the packing nodes with each other.

The details of the packing algorithm can be found in Appendix A.

Discourse structure

The discourse structure takes the form of a SDRS-like discourse representation, which we presented in section 3.4. It is completed by an event structure used for modeling temporal and aspectual information à la Moens and Steedman [1988].

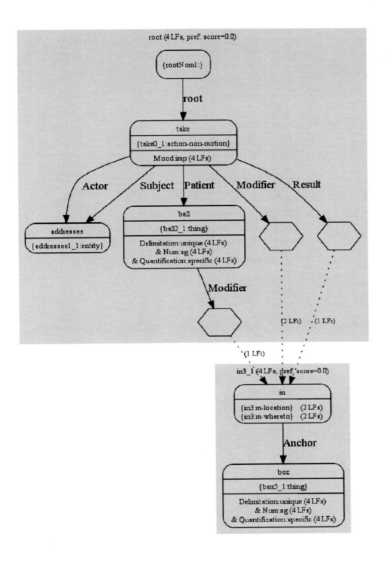

Figure 4.8: Example of packed logical form [PLF] for the utterance "Put the ball inside the box". Four distinct logical forms are contained in this representation. The PLF is made of two packing nodes (indicated by the grey area), connected with each other by three packing edges (indicated by the small polygons). In total, five packed nominals are included in the representation, plus one "dummy" root nominal which points to the head of the logical form. For each nominal, we specify (1) the logical proposition, (2) the ontological sort, and (3) the set of possible features.

59

rhetorical relations

dialogue move

Practically, the discourse structure is defined as a set of packed logical forms connected by *rhetorical relations* (e.g. EXPLANATION, NARRATION, ELABORATION, etc.). Since we are dealing with dialogue, these relations often represent *dialogue moves* (also called speech acts or conversational moves) [Traum, 1993; Poesio and Traum, 1997].

Name of dialogue move	Example
ASSERT	"The ball is red"
QUESTION-W	"Which ball is to the left of the box?"
QUESTION-YN	"Is this a ball?"
ACTION-DIRECTIVE	"Now take the red ball and put it in front of you"
ACCEPT	"Ok"
REJECT	"No that's wrong"
OPENING	"Hi robot"
CLOSING	"Goodbye!"

Table 4.1: List of recognised dialogue moves

cache

A *cache* is associated to each packed logical form in the discourse structure. This cache contains the set of discourse referents used in the PLF. Discourse referents can be connected *across* caches of PLFs in order to indicate that their associated linguistic expressions refer to the same entity. In other words, the connection between caches is used to represent *discourse referent resolution*.

nucleus

Finally, the event structure is modeled as a network of *nuclei*. A nucleus is a tripartite structure, consisting of a *"preparation"* (the activity bringing the event about), a *"culmination"* (the goal event), and a *"consequent"* (the state ensuing the event). The nuclei are directly connected to the discourse referents in the cache.

Figure 4.9 illustrates an example of full discourse structure. The schema is automatically generated at runtime by the module responsible for updating the discourse structure.

4.2.2 Processes

The communication subarchitecture can be roughly divided into four basic components (which are illustrated in Figure 4.4): the *speech recogniser*, the *incremental parser*, the *dialogue-level interpreter*, and finally the *connection with the other modalities*. See Figure 4.10 for a simplified time diagram illustrating the interactions between the four components.

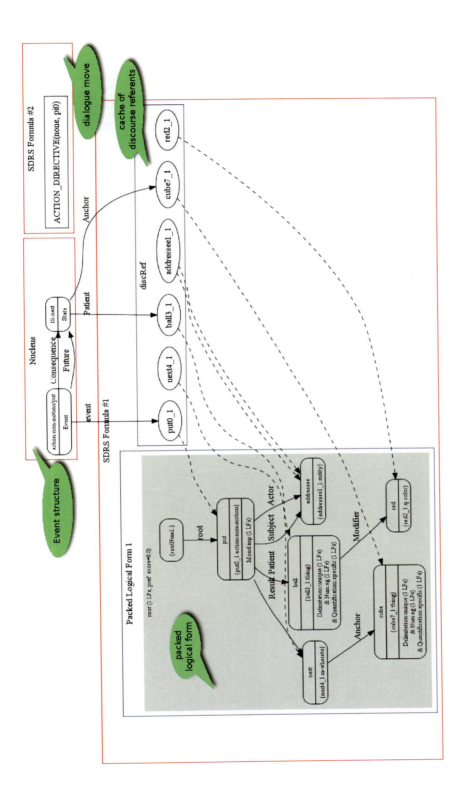

Figure 4.9: Example of packed logical form augmented with pragmatic interpretations. The analysed utterance is "put the green ball close to the cube". The rectangle with a red border includes the *packed logical form* as well as a *cache* listing the available discourse referents. Above this rectangle are two smaller rectangles. The left one represents the *event structure* of the utterance – it indicates that "putting the green ball close to the cube" is an event which, once accomplished, has for consequence that the ball is next to the cube. The rectangle on the right represents the interpreted *dialogue move* (or speech act) of the utterance: an ACTION-DIRECTIVE.

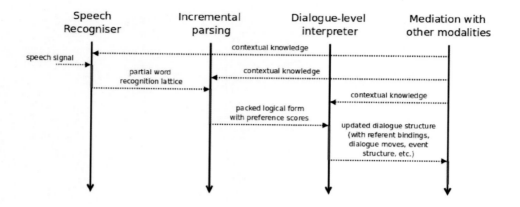

Figure 4.10: Simplified time diagram for the communication subarchitecture

1. Speech recognition

The speech recognition is based on Nuance Recognizer v8.5 together with a *statistical language model*, more precisely a class-based trigram language model. As we will see in Chapter 5, the probabilities included in the language model are constantly updated at runtime to adapt the system to changes in the environment.

word lattices

The speech recogniser outputs recognition hypotheses in the form of *word lattices*. The hypotheses yielded by the speech recogniser are *partial* hypotheses. We do not wait for the utterance to be complete to estimate the possible hypotheses. As soon as a sequence of words has been recognised in the speech stream, the ASR system computes a set of hypotheses for it, and sends the result to the rest of the system. These partial hypotheses are then progressively extended and refined as the utterance unfolds.

Once they are generated, the word lattices are inserted into the working memory of the subarchitecture, where they can be retrieved by the other components for further processing.

2. Incremental parsing

The parsing operations are factorized into several interconnected functions:

context-sensitive lexical retrieval

1 *Context-sensitive lexical retrieval*: As a new word is being recognised by the ASR, the first step is to retrieve a set of possible lexical entries from the lexicon. A lexicon entry specifies all possible syntactic and

semantic uses of a given word. The situated and task context can be exploited to restrict what lexical meanings can be retrieved.

2. *Incremental syntactic parsing*: Syntactic parsing is based on an incremental chart parser built on top of the OpenCCG NLP library[1] for **Combinatory Categorial Grammar**, which we have already described in Chapter 3.

Incremental syntactic parsing

The utterances are parsed in a word-by-word, left-to-right fashion, based on a *bottom-up CKY parser* [Ney, 1991]. At each step, the chart is updated with all possible partial analyses for the given utterance segment. These analyses represent the syntactic and semantic structure built for the utterance so far, and indicate possible ways in which these analyses can be continued by means of open arguments. Figure 4.11 illustrates a simple example of incremental parse.

After each incremental step, the parser checks whether it has reached a *frontier*. A frontier is specified as a type of complete grammatical structure at the right branch of a grammatical derivation. This enables us to specify whether the parser should return after every word, or e.g. after every phrase. At each frontier check, the chart is pruned using a category scorer. This scorer ranks the categories for the partial analyses construed so far, possibly pruning them if they are guaranteed not to lead to a complete analysis [Kruijff *et al.*, 2009].

Once all analyses are extracted, the parser yields a set of interpretations, expressed as HLDS *logical forms*.

logical forms

3. *Packing* and *pruning* of the construed analyses: a *packing* mechanism is used by the incremental parser to efficiently represent and manipulate logical forms across the communication subarchitecture. The packed logical form is then pruned to eliminate the interpretations which are not contextually supported. The packing algorithm is explained in more detail in Appendix A.

packing of logical forms

4. And finally, discriminative *parse selection*: as will be explained in detail in Chapter 6, a discriminative model is used to assign a likelihood score to each possible interpretation. The logical form with the highest score is then selected and inserted into the working memory for further processing. The discriminative model includes semantic, syntactic, acoustic and contextual features and is trained with a simple perceptron algorithm.

parse selection

---

[1] http://openccg.sf.net

63

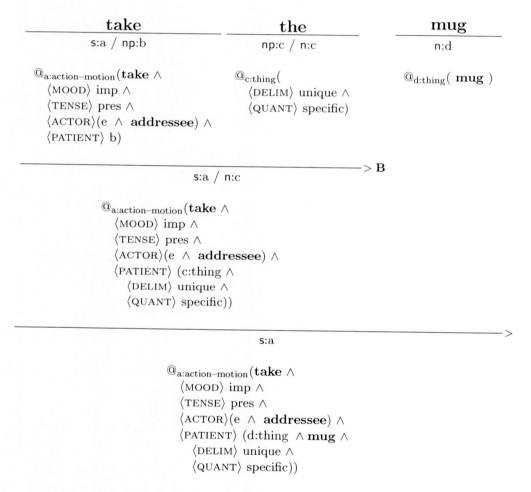

Figure 4.11: Incremental parsing of the utterance "take the mug".

3. Dialogue interpretation

Once the packed logical form is built, it is retrieved by the dialogue recognition module, which performs dialogue-level analysis tasks such as discourse reference resolution, dialogue move interpretation, event-structure recognition, and consequently updates the dialogue structure.

The *discourse reference resolution* module is responsible for the appropriate binding of referring expressions (deictics, demonstratives, pronouns, definite NPs) to their referent in the dialogue structure. This is done via a simple algorithm which searches in the dialogue history the most *salient* referent which meets the constraints imposed by the referring expressions. For our purposes, the linguistic saliency of a given referent is equivalent to its *recency* (that is, the number of utterances which separates the referent from the current position in the dialogue).

discourse reference resolution

Once the discourse reference resolution is performed, the anaphoric relations between the various discourse referents is specified by way of connections across the *caches* of the formulas which populate the discourse structure (cfr. previous section for the notion of cache).

The *dialogue move interpretation* is implemented with a *decision tree* exploring various linguistic features to determine the most likely dialogue move for a given utterance. For instance, the dialogue move ACTION-DIRECTIVE is defined with two simple features: a verb expressed in the *imperative form*, and whose ontological sort is an *action*.

dialogue move interpretation
decision tree

The recognised dialogue move is then integrated into the discourse structure, as a SDRT formula linking back to its associated packed logical form.

Finally, the *event structure recognition* is responsible for building up the nucleus associated to the utterance. The nodes inside the nucleus are linked to the discourse referents specified in the cache. Once the nucleus is created, it is connected to the full event structure (a network of nuclei which spans the complete discourse structure).

event structure recognition

Figure 4.9 illustrated a typical result of these discourse-level interpretations.

4. Cross-modal binding

Linguistic interpretations must finally be associated with extra-linguistic knowledge about the environment – dialogue comprehension hence needs to connect with other subarchitectures like vision, spatial reasoning or planning. We realise this information binding between different modalities via a specific module, called the *"binder"*, which is responsible for the ontology-based *mediation* across modalities [Jacobsson *et al.*, 2008].

ontology-based mediation

A component of particular importance for our purpose is the *multimodal salience modeling* tool. The role of this component is to extract a set of salient entities, both from the physical environment (objects present in the visual scene), and from the interaction itself (previously referred-to elements in the dialogue history). This contextual knowledge is then exploited to create a cross-modal *salience model*. Once computed, the salience model is inserted into the working memory, where it can be retrieved by the various components involved in dialogue comprehension and help guide the interpretation process. The next chapter explains in detail how the salience model is built up, and how it is integrated into the speech recogniser to prime the utterance recognition.

[margin note: salience model]

4.3 Summary of the chapter

This chapter described the *software architecture* on which our approach rests.

- We started with a brief outlook on the general *cognitive architecture* used in our robotic platform. We listed its main characteristics (distributed memory, parallel refinement of shared representations, control of information and processing, and ontology-based knowledge management). We also detailed the strategy followed by the architecture to address the *"binding problem"*.

- We then concentrated on the *communication* subarchitecture. We analysed the subarchitecture both in terms of *representations* and in terms of *processes* operating on these representations. These processes can be grouped into four groups, one for each major processing step:

    - The *speech recogniser* is responsible for the transformation of a speech signal into a word lattice expressing the various recognition hypotheses. This word lattice is continuously updated and extended as the utterance unfolds.

    - The *incremental parser* takes a word lattice as input, and outputs an ordered set of possible interpretations. These interpretations are expressed as a packed logical form along with associated preference scores (assigned by the discriminative model detailed in Chapter 6). The parser itself is based on an incremental CKY parser for Combinatory Categorial Grammar.

    - The *dialogue-level interpreter* integrates the packed logical forms into a discourse structure. It performs various dialogue-level tasks such as discourse referent resolution, dialogue move interpretation, and event structure recognition.

– Finally, the *cross-modal binding* is responsible for the mediation with the other modalities. Of particular interest is the *salience modeling* component, which builds up a cross-modal model of salient entities. This model can be used by various components to prime utterance comprehension with contextual knowledge.

Now that the necessary background knowledge has been laid out, we dive in the next two chapters into the details of our approach, starting with situated speech recognition.

Part II

Approach

5
Situated Speech Recognition

We present a model for speech recognition which relies on contextual information about salient entities to prime utterance recognition. The underlying hypothesis is that ASR performance can be significantly enhanced by exploiting knowledge about the immediate physical environment and the dialogue history. To this end, visual salience (objects perceived in the physical scene) and linguistic salience (previously referred-to objects in the current dialogue) are integrated into a unified cross-modal salience model. The model is dynamically updated as the environment evolves, and is used to establish expectations about uttered words which are most likely to be heard given the context. The update is realised by continuously adapting probabilities specified in the statistical language model. The chapter describes our approach in detail and reports the evaluation results on a test suite.

5.1 Introduction to the issue

Automatic speech recognition [ASR] is the first step in comprehending spoken dialogue. For robots operating in real-world noisy environments, and dealing with utterances pertaining to complex, open-ended domains, this step is particularly error-prone. In spite of continuous technological advances, the performance of ASR remains for most tasks at least an order of magnitude worse than that of human listeners [Moore, 2007].

One strategy for addressing this issue is to use context information to guide the speech recognition by percolating contextual constraints to the statistical language model [Gruenstein *et al.*, 2005]. In this chapter, we follow this approach by defining a *context-sensitive language model* which exploits information about salient objects in the visual scene and linguistic expressions in the dialogue history to prime recognition. To this end, a *salience*

<small>automatic speech recognition</small>

<small>context-sensitive language model</small>

model integrating both visual and linguistic salience is used to dynamically compute lexical activations, which are incorporated into the language model at runtime.

Our approach departs from previous work on context-sensitive speech recognition by modeling salience as inherently cross-modal, instead of relying on just one particular modality such as gesture [Chai and Qu, 2005], eye gaze [Qu and Chai, 2007] or dialogue state [Gruenstein et al., 2005]. The FUSE system described in [Roy and Mukherjee, 2005] is a closely related approach, but limited to the processing of object descriptions, whereas our system was designed from the start to handle generic situated dialogues (cfr. section 5.4).

The structure of this chapter[1] is as follows. After a brief reminder regarding the psycholinguistic motivation of our approach, we describe the cross-modal salience model we developed to model *situated context*. We then proceed by explaining how it is utilised within the language model used for ASR. Finally, we present the evaluation results of our approach.

5.2 Psycholinguistic motivation

As psycholinguistic studies have shown, humans do not process linguistic utterances in isolation from other modalities. Eye-tracking experiments notably highlighted that, during utterance comprehension, humans combine, in a closely time-locked fashion, *linguistic information* with *scene understanding* and *world knowledge* [Altmann and Kamide, 2004; Knoeferle and Crocker, 2006]. These observations – along with many others – therefore provide solid evidence for the *embodied* and *situated* nature of language and cognition [Lakoff, 1987; Barsalou, 1999].

Humans thus systematically exploit dialogue and situated context to guide attention and help disambiguate and refine linguistic input by filtering out unlikely interpretations. Our approach is essentially an attempt to improve the speech recognition by drawing inspiration from the contextual priming effects evidenced in human cognition.

5.3 Salience modeling

In our implementation, we define *salience* using two main sources of information:

---

[1]This chapter is a slightly adapted version of the paper presented at the ESSLLI 2008 Student Session [Lison, 2008], which took place in Hamburg on August 4-15, 2008.

1. the salience of objects in the perceived visual scene;
2. the linguistic salience or "recency" of linguistic expressions in the dialogue history.

Other sources of information could also be added, for instance the possible presence of gestures [Chai and Qu, 2005], eye gaze tracking [Qu and Chai, 2007], entities in large-scale space [Zender and Kruijff, 2007], or the integration of a task model – as salience generally depends on intentionality [Landragin, 2006].

5.3.1 Visual salience

Via the "binder", we can access the set of objects currently perceived in the visual scene. Each object is associated with a concept name (e.g. **printer**) and a number of features, for instance spatial coordinates or qualitative propreties like colour, shape or size.

Several features can be used to compute the salience of an object. The ones currently used in our implementation are (1) the object size and (2) its distance relative to the robot (i.e. spatial proximity). Other features could also prove to be helpful, like the reachability of the object or its distance from the point of visual focus – similarly to the spread of visual acuity across the human retina. To derive the visual salience value for each object, we assign a numeric value for the two variables, and then perform a weighted addition. The associated weights are determined via regression tests.

visual salience

It is worth noting that the choice of a particular measure for the visual saliency is heavily dependent on the application domain and the properties of the visual scene (typical number of objects, relative distances, recognition capacities of the vision system, angle of view, etc.). For the application domain in which we performed our evaluation (cfr. section 5.6), the experimental results turned out to be largely indifferent to the choice of a specific method of calculation for the visual saliency.

At the end of the processing, we end up with a set $\mathbf{E}_v$ of visual objects, each of which is associated with a numeric salience value $s(e_k)$, with $e_k \in \mathbf{E}_v$.

5.3.2 Linguistic salience

There is a vast amount of literature on the topic of linguistic salience. Roughly speaking, linguistic salience can be characterised either in terms of *hierarchical recency*, according to a tree-like model of discourse structure (cfr. Grosz and Sidner [1986]; Grosz *et al.* [1995]; Asher and Lascarides [2003]), or in terms of *linear recency* of mention (see Kelleher [2005] for a discussion). Our

linguistic salience

hierarchical/linear recency

Figure 5.1: Example of a visual scene

implementation can theoretically handle both types of linguistic salience, but for all practical purposes, the system only takes linear recency into account, as it is easier to compute and usually more reliable than hierarchical recency (which crucially depends on having a well-formed discourse structure).

To compute the linguistic salience, we extract a set $\mathbf{E}_l$ of potential referents from the discourse structure, and for each referent e_k we assign a salience value $s(e_k)$ equal to the distance (measured on a logarithmic scale) between its last mention and the current position in the discourse structure.

5.3.3 Cross-modal salience model

<small>cross-modal statistical model</small>

Once the visual and linguistic salience are computed, we can proceed to their integration into a *cross-modal statistical model*. We define the set $\mathbf{E}$ as the union of the visual and linguistic entities: $\mathbf{E} = \mathbf{E}_v \cup \mathbf{E}_l$, and devise a probability distribution $P(\mathbf{E})$ on this set:

$$P(e_k) = \frac{\delta_v\ I_{\mathbf{E}_v}(e_k)\ s_v(e_k)\ +\ \delta_l\ I_{\mathbf{E}_l}(e_k)\ s_l(e_k)}{|\mathbf{E}|} \qquad (5.1)$$

where $I_A(x)$ is the indicator function of set A, and δ_v, δ_l are factors controlling the relative importance of each type of salience. They are determined empirically, subject to the following constraint to normalise the distribution :

$$\delta_v \sum_{e_k \in \mathbf{E}_v} s(e_k) + \delta_l \sum_{e_k \in \mathbf{E}_l} s(e_k) = |\mathbf{E}| \qquad (5.2)$$

The statistical model $P(\mathbf{E})$ thus simply reflects the salience of each visual or linguistic entity: the more salient, the higher the probability.

5.4 Lexical activation

In order for the salience model to be of any use for speech recognition, a connection between the salient entities and their associated words in the ASR vocabulary needs to be established. To this end, we define a *lexical activation network*, which lists, for each possible salient entity, the set of words activated by it. The network specifies the words which are likely to be heard when the given entity is present in the environment or in the dialogue history. It can therefore include words related to the object denomination, subparts, common properties or affordances. The salient entity **laptop** will activate words like 'laptop', 'notebook', 'screen', 'opened', 'ibm', 'switch on/off', 'close', etc. The list is structured according to word classes, and a weight can be set on each word to modulate the lexical activation: supposing a **laptop** is present, the word 'laptop' should receive a higher activation than, say, the word 'close', which is less situation specific.

lexical activation network

The use of lexical activation networks is a key difference between our model and [Roy and Mukherjee, 2005], which relies on a measure of "descriptive fitness" to modify the word probabilities. One advantage of our approach is the possibility to go beyond object descriptions and activate word types denoting subparts, properties or affordances of objects. In the context of a **laptop** object, words such as 'screen', 'ibm', 'closed' or 'switch on/off' would for instance be activated.

If the probability of specific words is increased, we need to re-normalise the probability distribution. One solution would be to decrease the probability of all non-activated words accordingly. This solution, however, suffers from a significant drawback: our vocabulary contains many context-independent words like prepositions, determiners or general words like 'thing' or 'place', whose probability should remain constant. To address this issue, we mark an explicit distinction in our vocabulary between *context-dependent* and *context-independent* words. Only the context-dependent words can be activated or deactivated by the context. The context-independent words maintain a constant probability. Figure 5.2 illustrates these distinctions.

In the current implementation, the lexical activation network is constructed semi-manually, using a simple lexicon extraction algorithm. We start with the list of possible salient entities, which is given by:

1. the set of physical objects the vision system can recognise ;
2. the set of nouns specified in the CCG lexicon with 'object' as ontological type.

For each entity, we then extract its associated lexicon by matching domain-specific syntactic patterns against a corpus of dialogue transcripts.

Figure 5.2: Graphical illustration of the word activation network

5.5 Language modeling

language model

We now detail the language model used for the speech recognition – a class-based trigram model enriched with contextual information provided by the salience model.

5.5.1 Corpus generation

We need a corpus to train any statistical language model. Unfortunately, no corpus of situated dialogue adapted to our task domain is available to this day. Collecting in-domain data via Wizard of Oz experiments is a very costly and time-consuming process, so we decided to follow the approach advocated in [Weilhammer *et al.*, 2006] instead and generate a class-based corpus from a task grammar we had at our disposal.

Practically, we first collected a small set of WoZ experiments, totalling about 800 utterances. This set is of course too small to be directly used as a corpus for language model training, but sufficient to get an intuitive idea of the kind of utterances we had to deal with.

domain-specific grammar

Based on it, we designed a domain-specific context-free grammar able to cover most of the utterances. Weights were then automatically assigned to each grammar rule by parsing our initial corpus, hence leading to a small *stochastic context-free grammar*.

As a last step, this grammar is randomly traversed a large number of times, which yields the final corpus.

Additional details regarding the domain-specific grammar used for corpus generation can be found in Appendix C.

5.5.2 Salience-driven, class-based language models

The objective of the speech recognizer is to find the word sequence $\mathbf{W}^*$ which has the highest probability given the observed speech signal $\mathbf{O}$ and a set $\mathbf{E}$ of salient objects:

$$\mathbf{W}^* = \arg\max_{\mathbf{W}} P(\mathbf{W}|\mathbf{O}; \mathbf{E}) \tag{5.3}$$

$$= \arg\max_{\mathbf{W}} \underbrace{P(\mathbf{O}|\mathbf{W})}_{\text{acoustic model}} \times \underbrace{P(\mathbf{W}|\mathbf{E})}_{\text{salience-driven language model}} \tag{5.4}$$

For a trigram language model, the probability of the word sequence $P(w_1^n|\mathbf{E})$ is:

trigram language model

$$P(w_1^n|\mathbf{E}) \simeq \prod_{i=1}^{n} P(w_i|w_{i-1}w_{i-2}; \mathbf{E}) \tag{5.5}$$

Our language model is class-based, so it can be further decomposed into word-class and class transitions probabilities. The class transition probabilities reflect the language syntax; we assume they are independent of salient objects. The word-class probabilities, however, do depend on context: for a given class – e.g. *noun* -, the probability of hearing the word 'laptop' will be higher if a laptop is present in the environment. Hence:

class-based model

$$P(w_i|w_{i-1}w_{i-2}; \mathbf{E}) = \underbrace{P(w_i|c_i; \mathbf{E})}_{\text{word-class probability}} \times \underbrace{P(c_i|c_{i-1}, c_{i-2})}_{\text{class transition probability}} \tag{5.6}$$

We now define the word-class probabilities $P(w_i|c_i; \mathbf{E})$:

$$P(w_i|c_i; \mathbf{E}) = \sum_{e_k \in \mathbf{E}} P(w_i|c_i, e_k) \times P(e_k) \tag{5.7}$$

To compute $P(w_i|c_i, e_k)$, we use the lexical activation network specified for e_k:

77

$$P(w_i|c_i, e_k) = \begin{cases} P(w_i|c_i) + \alpha_1 & \text{if} \quad w_i \in \text{activatedWords}(e_k) \\ P(w_i|c_i) - \alpha_2 & \text{if} \quad w_i \notin \text{activatedWords}(e_k) \land \\ & \quad w_i \in \text{contextDependentWords} \\ P(w_i|c_i) & \text{else} \end{cases} \quad (5.8)$$

The optimum value of α_1 is determined using regression tests. α_2 is computed relative to α_1 in order to keep the sum of all probabilities equal to 1:

$$\alpha_2 = \frac{|\text{activatedWords}|}{|\text{contextDependentWords}| - |\text{activatedWords}|} \times \alpha_1$$

These word-class probabilities are dynamically updated as the environment and the dialogue evolves and incorporated into the language model at runtime.

5.6 Evaluation

5.6.1 Evaluation procedure

Wizard-of-Oz experiments

We evaluated our approach using a test suite of 250 spoken utterances recorded during Wizard-of-Oz experiments (a representative subset of the 800 utterances initially collected). The participants were asked to interact with the robot while looking at a specific visual scene. We designed 10 different visual scenes by systematic variation of the nature, number and spatial configuration of the objects presented. Figure 5.3 gives an example of visual scene.

The interactions could include descriptions, questions and commands. No particular tasks were assigned to the participants. The only constraint we imposed was that all interactions with the robot had to be related to the shared visual scene.

After being recorded, all spoken utterances have been manually segmented one-by-one, and transcribed.

5.6.2 Results

Table 5.1 summarises our experimental results. We focus our analysis on the WER of our model compared to the baseline – that is, compared to a class-based trigram model not based on salience.

The table details the WER results obtained by comparing the first recognition hypothesis to the gold standard transcription. Below these results,

Figure 5.3: Sample visual scene including three objects: a box, a ball, and a chocolate bar.

Word Error Rate [WER]:	Classical LM	Salience-driven LM
vocabulary size $\simeq$ *200 words*	25.04 % (NBest 3: 20.72 %)	24.22 % (NBest 3: 19.97 %)
vocabulary size $\simeq$ *400 words*	26.68 % (NBest 3: 21.98 %)	**23.85** % (NBest 3: 19.97 %)
vocabulary size $\simeq$ *600 words*	28.61 % (NBest 3: 24.59 %)	23.99 % (NBest 3: 20.27 %)

Table 5.1: Comparative results of recognition performance

we also indicate the results obtained with NBest 3 – that is, the results obtained by considering the first three recognition hypotheses (instead of the first one). The word error rate is then computed as the *minimum* value of the word error rates yielded by the three hypotheses[2].

---

[2]Or to put it slightly differently, the word error rate for NBest 3 is computed by

5.6.3 Analysis

As the results show, the use of a salience model can enhance the recognition performance in situated interactions: with a vocabulary of about 600 words, the WER is indeed reduced by $\frac{28.61-23.99}{28.61} \times 100 = \mathbf{16.1}$ % compared to the baseline. According to the *Sign* test, the differences for the last two tests (400 and 600 words) are statistically significant. As we could expect, the salience-driven approach is especially helpful when operating with a larger vocabulary, where the expectations provided by the salience model can really make a difference in the word recognition.

The word error rate remains nevertheless quite high. This is due to several reasons. The major issue is that the words causing most recognition problems are – at least in our test suite – function words like prepositions, discourse markers, connectives, auxiliaries, etc., and not content words. Unfortunately, the use of function words is usually not context-dependent, and hence not influenced by salience. By classifying the errors according to the part-of-speech of the misrecognised word, we estimated that 89 % of the recognition errors were due to function words. Moreover, our test suite is constituted of "free speech" interactions, which often include lexical items or grammatical constructs outside the range of our language model.

5.7 Summary of the chapter

We have presented an implemented model for speech recognition based on the concept of *salience*. This salience is defined via *visual* and *linguistic* cues, and is used to compute degrees of *lexical activations*, which are in turn applied to dynamically adapt the ASR *language model* to the robot's environment and dialogue state. The obtained experimental results demonstrate the effectiveness of our approach.

It is worth noting that the primary role of the context-sensitive ASR mechanism outlined in this chapter is to establish *expectations* about uttered words which are most likely to be heard given the context – that is, to *anticipate* what will be uttered. In the next chapter, we move a step further, and explain how we can also use the context as a *discrimination* tool to select the most relevant interpretations of a given utterance.

---

assuming that, out of the three suggested recognition hypotheses, the one finally selected is always the one with the minimal error.

6
Robust Parsing of Spoken Dialogue

We present in this chapter the approach we developed for the robust parsing of spoken inputs. After a general overview, we start by describing the grammar relaxation mechanism devised to parse slightly ill-formed or misrecognised utterances. We then go on to detail the discriminative model used to select the most likely parses among the ones allowed by the relaxed grammar. We explain what a discriminative model is, and how it can be applied to our task. We then describe the learning algorithm, the training data, and the various features on which the discriminative model operates. We conclude this chapter by explaining two interesting extensions of our approach.

Parsing spoken inputs is a notoriously difficult task. The parser must be made robust to both speech recognition errors and ill-formed utterances, such as those including disfluencies (pauses, speech repairs, repetitions, corrections), ellipsis, fragments, a- or extra-grammatical constructions. Three broad families of techniques are generally used in the literature to tackle this problem:

robust parsing of spoken inputs

1. The first family includes the large set of **shallow** or **partial parsing** techniques such as *"concept spotting"*. In this approach, a small hand-crafted, task-specific grammar is used to extract specific constituents and turn these into basic semantic concepts [Dowding *et al.*, 1994; Allen *et al.*, 1996]. These techniques are usually quite efficient, but are also highly domain-specific, fragile, and requires a lot of development and optimisation effort.

shallow parsing

2. **Statistical approaches** are also widely used for robust parsing. They can take the form of either (1) flat models derived from Hidden Markov Models [Pieraccini *et al.*, 1992], or (2) structured models relying on

stochastic parsing [Fine, 1998; Collins, 1997; Charniak, 2001; He and Young, 2005]. In both cases, the possible parses of a given utterance are computed based on the selection of the *most probable optimal coverage*. Pure statistical techniques have the advantage of being inherently robust, and can be trained automatically with annotated corpus data. Unfortunately, they are usually unable to deliver deep and detailed analysis [Rosé and Lavie, 2001], and have a large search space [Carroll and Briscoe, 1996; Ailomaa, 2004]. And of course, they are only applicable as long as there is available *training data* (i.e. annotated corpora) for the task domain.

3. The third family of techniques relies on the **controlled relaxation of grammar rules** [van Noord *et al.*, 1999; Chanod, 2000]. Contrary to (pure) stochastic parsing, grammar relaxation approaches are able to provide *deep* syntactic analyses. They however require more development time to build up the necessary grammatical resources[1]. The relaxation mechanism must also be carefully controlled in order to avoid a combinatory explosion of the number of parses.

The approach we present in this chapter belongs to the latter set of techniques, and contains several new improvements compared to the state of the art. It is based on a *grammar relaxation mechanism* coupled with a *discriminative model* selecting the most appropriate parse(s), a strategy we borrow from [Zettlemoyer and Collins, 2007]. The approach relies on a *hybrid* symbolic/statistical architecture and integrates *acoustic*, *semantic*, *syntactic* and *contextual* knowledge into a unified model.

The grammar relaxation mechanism is implemented by introducing *non-standards CCG rules* that relax certain parts of the grammar, for example allowing for the insertion of missing words, the treatment of disfluencies, the combination of distinct discourse units, or the correction of common speech recognition errors. Grammar relaxation has the potential to significantly increase the grammar coverage, but at a cost: the multiplication of the number of alternative parses.

A **parse selection** component (which we implement via a *discriminative model*) is hence integrated into the system in order to discriminate the correct parses from the incorrect ones, by "penalising" to a correct extent the relaxed grammatical analyses[2].

---

[1] Excepted when these grammatical resources are automatically extracted from corpora, see e.g. [Zettlemoyer and Collins, 2007]

[2] See also Raymond and Mooney [2006] concerning discriminative reranking methods for semantic parsing.

It is also worth noting that the integration of a parse selection component has the added advantage of associating an explicit **score** (or probability) to each parse. This score is a very worthy piece of information on its own, which can be used in various ways: for instance, it could be applied to trigger *clarification requests*, if it appears that no parse has a sufficient score (compared to a given threshold), or if several parses end up with a (quasi-)similar score. It can also be used during the *incremental parsing* to prune low-probability partial parses from the chart.

likelihood score

The rest of the chapter is as follows. We first present the grammar relaxation mechanism. We then proceed with a description of the discriminative model, detailing its formal properties, the learning algorithm and the associated training data. We also describe the set of linguistic and contextual features on which the model operates. We finally present two possible extensions of our approach.

6.1 Grammar relaxation

Our approach to robust processing of spoken dialogue rests on the idea of **grammar relaxation**: the grammatical constraints specified in the grammar are "relaxed" to handle slightly ill-formed or misrecognised utterances.

grammar relaxation

Practically, the grammar relaxation is done via the introduction of *non-standard CCG rules* [Zettlemoyer and Collins, 2007]. In Combinatory Categorial Grammar, rules are used to assemble categories to form larger pieces of syntactic and semantic structure. The standard rules are application $(<,>)$, composition (**B**), and type raising (**T**) [Steedman and Baldridge, 2009][3].

non-standard CCG rules

Using more powerful grammar rules to relax grammatical analysis in parsing tends, however, to increase the number of parses. We hence need a mechanism to discriminate among the possible parses - this is precisely the task of the discriminative model, which we will detail in section 6.2. But we first describe the non-standard rules we introduced.

6.1.1 New type-shifting rules

Following [Zettlemoyer and Collins, 2007], we introduce two new type-shifting rules in our grammar.

type-shifting rules

1. *Role-hypothesising type-shifting rule*:

    Imagine we encounter the utterance "put it the box", which is not parsable using our CCG grammar. A preposition, presumably 'in', is obviously

---

[3]See also Wittenburg [1987]; Hoyt and Baldridge [2008] for more advanced rules.

missing. This kind of phenomena can happen frequently, due for instance to speech recognition errors.

We can specify a new type-shifting rule in our grammar to handle this phenomena, which we shall call *role-hypothesising type-shifting rule* (labeled by $\mathbf{T}_R$):

$$\mathsf{np} : @_j c \Rightarrow \mathsf{pp} : @_{\{i:s\}} (p \wedge (\langle \textsc{Anchor} \rangle\, j \wedge c)) \qquad \boxed{\mathbf{T}_R}$$

where p is instantiated by a specific proposition and s a specific ontological sort. They usually represent the semantics of some preposition.

For example, if $p \leftarrow \mathbf{in}$ and $s \leftarrow \{\text{where–to}\}$, the rule becomes:

$$\mathsf{np} : @_j c \Rightarrow \mathsf{pp} : @_{\{i:\text{where–to}\}} (\mathbf{in} \wedge (\langle \textsc{Anchor} \rangle\, j \wedge c)) \qquad \boxed{\mathbf{T}_R(in)}$$

Figure 6.1 illustrates a parse using the rule $\mathbf{T}_R(in)$ (unnecessary details are omitted).

In order to prevent a combinatory explosion in the number of parses, the rule $\mathbf{T}_R$ is only instantiated to a small number of prepositions, like 'in' or 'to' – those which are causing most parsing failures.

2. *Null-head type-shifting rule*

The second type-shifting rule that we introduce is called the *null-head type-shifting rule*. Imagine we want to parse "take the blue in the box". Here again, there is a word presumably missing. We can introduce a new rule $\mathbf{T}_N$ to avoid this problem:

$$\mathsf{n} \backslash \mathsf{n} \vee \mathsf{n}/\mathsf{n} : @_j c \Rightarrow \mathsf{n} : @_{\{j:s\}} (p \wedge c) \qquad \boxed{\mathbf{T}_N}$$

where p and s are again instantiated to some specific proposition and ontological sort. These usually represent broad semantic categories, like a "thing", an "entity" or a "location". For example, if we instantiate $s \leftarrow \text{thing}$ and $p \leftarrow \mathbf{thing}$, the resulting rule $\mathbf{T}_N(thing)$ is:

$$\mathsf{n} \backslash \mathsf{n} \vee \mathsf{n}/\mathsf{n} : @_j c \Rightarrow \mathsf{n} : @_{\{j:\text{thing}\}} (\mathbf{thing} \wedge c)) \qquad \boxed{\mathbf{T}_N(thing)}$$

Figure 6.2 illustrates a successful parse using this rule.

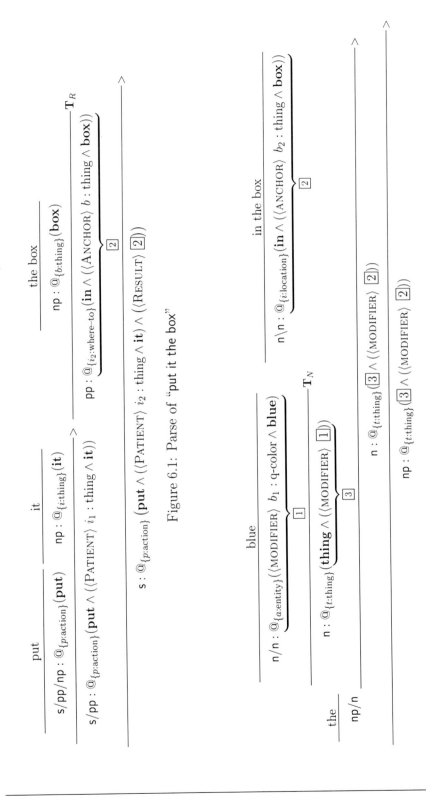

Figure 6.1: Parse of "put it the box"

Figure 6.2: Parse of "the blue in the box"

6.1.2 Paradigmatic heap rules

We also experimented with rules related to the notion of "*paradigmatic heap*", introduced in Chapter 2. Two types of syntactic relations are distinguished: *syntagmatic* relations and *paradigmatic* relations. Syntagmatic constructions are primarily characterized by *hypotactic* (i.e. head-dependent) relations between their constituents, whereas paradigmatic ones do not have such head-dependent asymmetry. Together, constituents connected by such paradigmatic relations form what Blanche-Benveniste et al. [1990] calls a "*paradigmatic heap*". A paradigmatic heap is defined as the position in a utterance where the "syntagmatic unfolding is interrupted", and the same syntactic position hence occupied by several linguistic objects. Disfluencies can be conveniently analysed as paradigmatic heaps.

Let us consider as a motivating example the following utterance (taken from the Apollo corpus):

(6.1) "it it probably shows up as a bright crater a bright crater on your map"

which can be conveniently analysed with the notion of "paradigmatic heap":

(6.2)
it
it   probably shows up as   a bright crater
                             a bright crater on your map

The rule $\mathbf{T}_{PH}$ is a type-changing rule which allows us to formalise the concept of paradigmatic heap in terms of a CCG rule, by "piling up" two constituents on a heap.

$$\mathsf{A} : @_a x \Rightarrow \mathsf{A} : @_c z \,/\, \mathsf{A} : @_b y \qquad \boxed{\mathbf{T}_{PH}}$$

where the formula $@_c z$ is defined as:

$$@_{\{c:\text{heap-units}\}}(\textbf{heap} \wedge \\ (\langle \text{FIRST} \rangle \; a \wedge x) \wedge \\ (\langle \text{NEXT} \rangle \; b \wedge y)) \qquad (6.3)$$

The category A stands for any category for which we want to allow this piling-up operation.

It is worth noting that in the rule $\mathbf{T}_{PH}$, the associated semantics of all elements contained in the heap is retained. This is desirable in certain conditions (i.e. when the elements in the heap complement each other), but for some disfluencies such as repetitions or corrections, we might want to only retain the semantic information of the last element, and discard the others[4]. An interesting forthcoming work would be to investigate how such distinction could be implemented in the rule system of a CCG grammar.

6.1.3 Discourse-level composition rules

In natural spoken dialogue, we may encounter utterances containing several independent "chunks" without any explicit separation (or only a short pause or a slight change in intonation), such as

(6.4) "ok robot, now take the ball - no, not this one, the other one - take the ball on your left... okay that's right, and now put it in the box."

Even if retrieving a fully structured parse for this utterance is difficult to achieve, it would be useful to have access to a list of smaller "discourse units". Syntactically speaking, a discourse unit can be any type of saturated atomic categories - from a simple discourse marker to a full sentence.

The type raising rule $\mathbf{T}_{du}$ allows the conversion of atomic categories into discourse units:

$$\mathsf{A} : @_i f \Rightarrow \mathsf{du} : @_i f \qquad (\mathbf{T}_{du})$$

where A represents an arbitrary saturated atomic category.

Rule $\mathbf{T}_C$ then integrates two discourse units into a single structure:

$$\mathsf{du} : @_a x \Rightarrow \mathsf{du} : @_c z \ / \ \mathsf{du} : @_b y \qquad (\mathbf{T}_C)$$

where the formula $@_c z$ is defined as:

$$@_{\{c:\text{d-units}\}}(\mathbf{list} \land \\
(\langle \text{FIRST} \rangle \ a \land x) \land \\
(\langle \text{NEXT} \rangle \ b \land y)) \qquad (6.5)$$

6.1.4 ASR error correction rules

Speech recognition is a highly error-prone task. It is however possible to partially alleviate this problem by inserting new **error-correction rules** (more precisely, new lexical entries) for the most frequently misrecognised words.

---

[4] As pointed out by Jason Baldridge (p.c.), such kind of combination would be analogous to the combinator **K** (vacuous abstraction).

If we notice for instance that the ASR system frequently substitutes the word 'wrong' for the word 'round' during the recognition (since they are phonologically close to each other), we can introduce a new lexical entry in the lexicon in order to correct this error:

$$\text{round} \vdash \text{adj} : @_{attitude}(\textbf{wrong}) \qquad \boxed{\textbf{lex}_{\{\text{round}\}}}$$

In total, thirteen new lexical entries of this type have been added to our lexicon to account for the most frequent recognition errors. The insertion of these lexical entries has been done manually, by analysing the output of the speech recogniser in order to detect the most frequent errors.

An interesting extension of our approach for the future would be to investigate whether this process can be automated and integrated within the learning algorithm itself. The biggest issue in this case would be to avoid an explosion of the search space.

6.1.5 Control of grammar relaxation

In order to avoid slowing down the dialogue comprehension system with the grammar relaxation, we integrated in the parser a simple control mechanism designed to limit the application of the relaxation rules.

The implemented mechanism is very simple: in each syntactic category construed by the parser, we keep track of the number of non-standard rules already applied in the category. If this number is above a given threshold (usually set to a maximum of 1 or 2 applications), we *suspend* the application of any new non-standard rules on this category. Of course, the constraint percolates from the lower categories to the higher ones enclosing them. This mechanism ensures that the grammar relaxation mechanism remains tractable. The threshold limiting the number of applications of non-standard rules can be easily modified, in order to allow for a stronger or weaker relaxation of the grammatical rules.

6.2 Discriminative models for parse selection

Once all the possible parses for a given utterance are computed, they must be subsequently filtered or selected in order to retain only the most likely interpretation(s). This is done via a (discriminative) statistical model covering a large number of features. This task of selecting the most likely interpretation among a set of possible ones is called *parse selection*.

6.2.1 Definition of the task

Formally, the task is defined as a function $F : \mathcal{X} \to \mathcal{Y}$ where the domain $\mathcal{X}$ is the set of possible inputs (in our case, $\mathcal{X}$ is the set of possible *word lattices*), and $\mathcal{Y}$ the set of parses. We assume:

parse selection

1. A function $\mathbf{GEN}(x)$ which enumerates all possible parses for an input x. In our case, this function simply represents the set of parses of x which are admissible according to the CCG grammar.

2. A d-dimensional feature vector $\mathbf{f}(x,y) \in \Re^d$, representing specific features of the pair (x,y). It can include various acoustic, syntactic, semantic or contextual features which may be relevant in discriminating the parses according to their likelihood.

3. A parameter vector $\mathbf{w} \in \Re^d$.

The function F, mapping a word lattice to its most likely parse, is then defined as:

$$F(x) = \underset{y \in \mathbf{GEN}(x)}{\operatorname{argmax}} \mathbf{w}^T \cdot \mathbf{f}(x,y) \qquad (6.6)$$

where $\mathbf{w}^T \cdot \mathbf{f}(x,y)$ is the inner product $\sum_{s=1}^{d} w_s\ f_s(x,y)$, and can be seen as a measure of the "quality" of the parse. Given the parameters $\mathbf{w}$, the optimal parse of a given utterance x can be therefore easily determined by enumerating all the parses generated by the grammar, extracting their features, computing the inner product $\mathbf{w}^T \cdot \mathbf{f}(x,y)$, and selecting the parse with the highest score.

The model defined by the parameters $\mathbf{w}$ in Equation (6.6) is also called a *linear model*, since the score assigned to each parse is computed as a *linear combination* of the feature values.

linear model

Parse selection is an example of *structured classification problem*, which is the problem of predicting an output y from an input x, where the output y has a rich internal structure. In the specific case of parse selection, x is a word lattice, and y a logical form.

structured classification

6.2.2 A distribution-free approach

Parameter estimation is the task of setting the parameter values $\mathbf{w}$ using the training data as evidence. How can we achieve that? The approach we take in this thesis is to use a *discriminative, distribution-free* (i.e. nonparametric) estimation method, implemented in a simple perceptron algorithm (described

parameter estimation

in the next section). This class of learning algorithms offers several distinctive advantages over the usual parametric techniques, which we shall now briefly discuss.

Let us assume a general framework for supervised learning, with an input domain $\mathcal{X}$ and an output domain $\mathcal{Y}$, where the task is to learn the mapping between $\mathcal{X}$ and $\mathcal{Y}$ based on a set of training examples. Two broad family of approaches are then conceivable[5]:

parametric models

- *Parametric models* attempt to solve the supervised learning problem by explicitly modeling either the joint distribution $D(x,y)$, or the conditional distributions $D(y|x)$ for all variables x. The crucial assumption is that there is some set of parameters $\Theta^* \in \Omega$ such that $D(x,y) = P(x,y|\Theta^*)$. In other words, we assume that $D(x,y)$ is a member of the set of distributions under consideration.

  Provided we have a training set $\{(x_1, y_1), ...(x_m, y_m)\}$ drawn from $D(x,y)$, a common estimation method is to set the parameters to the *maximum-likelihood estimates*, $\hat{\Theta} = \mathrm{argmax}_{\Theta \in \Omega} \, log P(x_i, y_i | \Theta)$.

  Maximum-likelihood estimation on parametric models must operate under quite strong assumptions – the most important one being that the structure of the statistical process generating the data is *known*. For instance, maximum-likelihood estimation for PCFGs is justified provided that the data was actually generated by a PCFG.

- *Distribution-free methods*, on the other hand, work on the weaker assumption that training and test examples are generated from the same distribution, but that the *form* of the distribution is unknown. These methods eschew the explicit modeling of the underlying distribution over all variables, and instead attempt to compute the mapping between input and output directly.

  Let's assume a loss function $L(y, \hat{y})$ expressing the cost of proposing an output $\hat{y}$ when the "true" output is y. A commonly used cost is the 0-1 loss $L(y, \hat{y}) = 0$ if $y = \hat{y}$ and $L(y, \hat{y}) = 1$ otherwise. Given a hypothesis function h mapping elements from $\mathcal{X}$ to $\mathcal{Y}$, its *expected loss* is defined as:

$$Er(h) = \sum_{x,y} D(x,y) L(y, h(x)) \qquad (6.7)$$

---

[5]The rest of the discussion is borrowed from [Collins, 2004].

$Er(h)$ is a measure of how successful the function h is. Unfortunately, we cannot explicitly calculate the expected loss of a hypothesis, since we do not have a direct access to the distribution $D(x,y)$, Using a training set of m pairs $\{(x_1, y_1), ...(x_m, y_m)\}$ – which are assumed to be drawn from $D(x,y)$ –, the *empirical loss* of the function h on the training sample is then defined as

$$\hat{Er}(h) = \frac{1}{m} \sum_i L(y_i, h(x_i)) \qquad (6.8)$$

The basic idea of distribution-free methods is to perform the parameter estimation directly from data so that its empirical loss is minimized [Vapnik, 1998].

$$\hat{h} = \underset{h \in \mathcal{H}}{\operatorname{argmin}} \hat{Er}(h) = \underset{h \in \mathcal{H}}{\operatorname{argmin}} \frac{1}{m} \sum_i L(y_i, h(x_i)) \qquad (6.9)$$

where $\hat{h}$ is the chosen hypothesis for the mapping between $\mathcal{X}$ and $\mathcal{Y}$.

The minimisation of the empirical loss is usually translated into the minimisation of an *error margin* in some high-dimensional space.

The perceptron algorithm that we present in the next section is an instance of such distribution-free methods. The algorithm is mathematically very elegant, and is able to deliver impressive experimental results. The theoretical underpinning of the approach in statistical learning theory is discussed at length in [Vapnik, 1998; Collins, 2004].

6.3 Learning

6.3.1 Training data

In order to estimate the parameters **w**, we need a set of training examples. Unfortunately, no corpus of situated dialogue adapted to our task domain is available to this day, let alone semantically annotated. The strategy we followed was therefore to extend the small domain-specific grammar described in section 5.5.1, in order to generate automatically a set of training examples.

Practically, we first collected a small set of WoZ data, totalling about a thousand utterances. Based on it, we designed a domain-specific context-free grammar able to cover most of the utterances. Each rule is associated to a semantic HLDS representation. Weights are automatically assigned to each grammar rule by parsing our initial corpus, hence leading to a small *stochastic context-free grammar* augmented with semantic information.

Once the grammar is specified, it is randomly traversed a large number of times, resulting in a large set (about 25.000) of utterances along with their semantic representations. Since we are interested in handling errors arising from speech recognition, we also need to "simulate" the most frequent recognition errors. To this end, we *synthesise* each string generated by the domain-specific CFG grammar, using a text-to-speech engine[6], feed the audio stream to the speech recogniser, and retrieve the recognition result. Via this technique, we are able to easily collect a large amount of training data.

Note that, instead of annotating entire derivations, we only specify the resulting *semantics* of the utterance, i.e. its logical form. The training data is thus represented by a set of examples (x_i, z_i), where x_i is an utterance and z_i is a HLDS formula. For a given training example (x_i, z_i), there may be several possible CCG parses which lead to the same semantics z_i. The estimation of the parameters based on the set of examples (x_i, z_i) can therefore be seen as a *hidden-variable* problem , where the training examples contain only partial information.

The context-specific grammar used to generate the training data is described in more detail in Appendix C.

6.3.2 Averaged perceptron

The algorithm we use to estimate the parameters **w** using the training data is a **perceptron**. The algorithm is fully online - it visits each example in turn and updates **w** if necessary. Albeit simple, the algorithm has proven to be very efficient and accurate for the task of parse selection [Collins and Roark, 2004; Collins, 2004; Zettlemoyer and Collins, 2005, 2007].

The pseudo-code for the online learning algorithm is detailed in [**Algorithm 1**].

It works as follows: the parameters **w** are first initialised to some arbitrary values. Then, for each pair (x_i, z_i) in the training set, the algorithm searches for the parse y' with the highest score according to the current model. If this parse happens to match the best parse which generates z_i (which we shall denote y^*), we move to the next example. Else, we perform a simple perceptron update on the parameters:

$$\mathbf{w} = \mathbf{w} + \mathbf{f}(x_i, y^*) - \mathbf{f}(x_i, y') \qquad (6.10)$$

The iteration on the training set is repeated T times, or until convergence.

---

[6]We used MARY (http://mary.dfki.de) for the text-to-speech engine.

Note that the most expensive step in this algorithm is the calculation of $y' = \mathrm{argmax}_{y \in \mathbf{GEN}(x_i)} \mathbf{w}^T \cdot \mathbf{f}(x_i, y)$ - this is the *decoding* problem.

It is possible to prove that, provided the training set (x_i, z_i) is separable with margin $\delta > 0$, the algorithm is assured to converge after a finite number of iterations to a model with zero training errors [Collins and Roark, 2004]. See also [Collins, 2004] for convergence theorems and proofs.

Following [Collins, 2002], we compute the *average* of the parameters once the learning is complete. Let $\mathbf{w}_i^t$ be the parameter vector after the ith example on the t pass through the data. Then the averaged parameter vector is

$$\mathbf{w}_{average} = \sum_{t=1}^{T} \sum_{i=1}^{n} \frac{\mathbf{w}_i^t}{nT} \qquad (6.11)$$

This averaging method was shown to give substantial improvements in accuracy [Collins, 2002].

6.3.3 Decoding

The decoding operation is the search for the most likely parse y^* for the word lattice x:

$$y^* = \underset{y \in \mathbf{GEN}(x)}{\mathrm{argmax}} \mathbf{w}^T \cdot \mathbf{f}(x, y) \qquad (6.12)$$

decoding

This operation is computationally expensive since the set of possible parses $\mathbf{GEN}(x)$ can grow exponentially with the length of x. The grammatical constraints specified in the CCG grammar can substantially reduce the size of $\mathbf{GEN}(x)$, but for ambiguous or complicated sentences, we may still end up with hundreds of different parses.

Some approaches (e.g. Zettlemoyer and Collins [2005]) use a beam-search algorithm to compute the value of (6.12). Beam search, like other dynamic programming techniques, requires the features $\mathbf{f}(x, y)$ to be strictly *local*, which is not the case for many of our features. For instance, the adequacy of an hypothesised dialogue move relative to the discourse context is a *global* feature of the whole utterance, not of a single word. This is also the case for the dependency relations included in the semantic features.

We therefore need to find other ways to implement the computations in (6.12) efficiently. This is where the *packed logical form* representation incorporated in our architecture proves to be extremely helpful. Instead of computing the feature vector $\mathbf{f}(x, y)$ for each parse y separately, we take advantage of the efficient "information packaging" provided by the packed logical form, and compute the semantic features directly on this structure.

Algorithm 1 Online perceptron learning

Require: - Examples is a set of n training examples $\{(x_i, z_i) : i = 1...n\}$
- T is the number of iterations over the training set
- GEN(x) is a function enumerating all possible parses for an input x, according to the CCG grammar.
- GEN(x, z) is a function enumerating all possible parses for an input x and which has semantics z, according to the CCG grammar.
- $L(y)$ maps a parse tree y to its associated logical form.
- Initial parameter vector $\mathbf{w_0}$

% *Initialise*
$\mathbf{w} \leftarrow \mathbf{w_0}$

% *Loop T times on the training examples*
for $t = 1...T$ **do**
  for $i = 1...n$ **do**

    % *Compute best parse according to current model*
    Let $y' = \mathrm{argmax}_{y \in \mathbf{GEN}(x_i)}\, \mathbf{w}^T \cdot \mathbf{f}(x_i, y)$

    % *If the decoded parse $\neq$ expected parse, update the parameters*
    if $L(y') \neq z_i$ **then**

      % *Search the best parse for utterance x_i with semantics z_i*
      Let $y^* = \mathrm{argmax}_{y \in \mathbf{GEN}(x_i, z_i)}\, \mathbf{w}^T \cdot \mathbf{f}(x_i, y)$

      % *Update parameter vector $\mathbf{w}$*
      Set $\mathbf{w} = \mathbf{w} + \mathbf{f}(x_i, y^*) - \mathbf{f}(x_i, y')$

      % *Record current values of $\mathbf{w}$*
      Set $\mathbf{w_i^t} = \mathbf{w}$
    end if

  end for
end for

% *Compute average and return the learned parameters*
$\mathbf{w} = \sum_{t=1}^{T} \sum_{i=1}^{n} \frac{\mathbf{w}_i^t}{nT}$

return parameter vector $\mathbf{w}$

All the semantic features $\mathbf{f}(x, y)$ are therefore computed directly, *in one pass*, by traversing the packed representation.

6.4 Features

As we have seen, the parse selection operates by enumerating the possible parses and selecting the one with the highest score according to the linear model parametrised by $\mathbf{w}$.

The accuracy of our method crucially relies on the selection of "good" features $\mathbf{f}(x, y)$ for our model - that is, features which help *discriminating* the parses. They must also be relatively cheap to compute. In our model, the features are of four types: semantic features, syntactic features, contextual features, and speech recognition features.

features of the discriminative model

6.4.1 Semantic features

What are the substructures of a logical form which can be relevant to discriminate the parses? A logical form (a typical example is illustrated in Figure 6.3) being essentially defined as a set of nominals connected by dependency relations, we can define features on these information sources:

semantic features

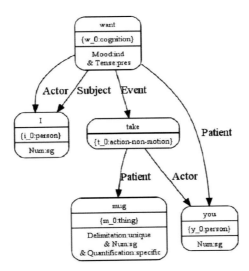

Figure 6.3: Graphical representation of the logical form for "I want you to take the mug" (the full HLDS formula is presented in 4.6).

1. *Nominals*: for each possible pair $\langle prop, sort \rangle$, we include a feature f_i in $\mathbf{f}(x,y)$ counting the number of nominals with ontological sort *sort* and proposition *prop* in the logical form.

2. *Ontological sorts*: features counting the occurrences of specific ontological sorts in the logical form.

3. *Dependency relations*: following [Clark and Curran, 2003], we also model the *dependency structure* of the logical form. Each dependency relation is defined as a triple $\langle sort_a, sort_b, label \rangle$, where $sort_a$ denotes the ontological sort of the incoming nominal, $sort_b$ the sort of the outgoing nominal, and *label* is the relation label.

4. *Sequences of dependency relations*: We also count the number of occurrences of particular sequences (i.e. bigram counts) of dependency relations.

5. *Existence of at least one well-formed parse*: Finally, we also include a feature specifying whether the utterance is parsable or not (i.e. if it generates at least one well-formed parse). The objective here is to favour the recognition hypotheses which are parsable over those who are not.

The features on nominals and ontological sorts aim at modeling (aspects of) *lexical semantics* - e.g. which meanings are the most frequent for a given word -, whereas the features on relations and sequence of relations focus on *sentential semantics* - which dependencies are the most frequent.

ambiguities

In other words, these features help us handle *lexical* and *syntactic ambiguities*.

6.4.2 Syntactic features

derivational history

By "syntactic features", we mean features associated to the *derivational history* of a specific parse. The main use of these features is to *penalise* to a correct extent the application of the non-standard rules introduced into the grammar.

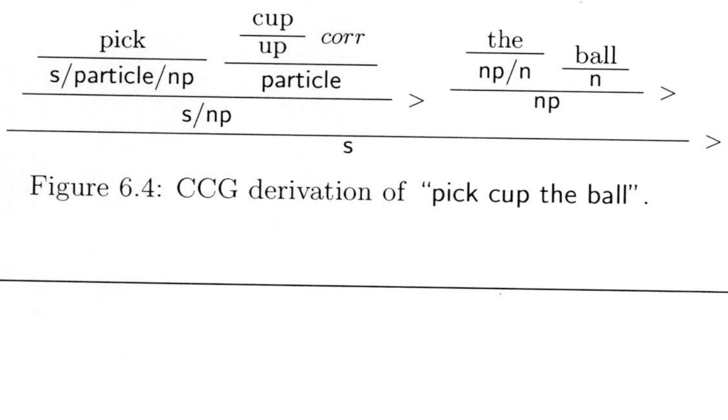

$$\frac{\dfrac{\text{pick}}{\text{s/particle/np}} \quad \dfrac{\dfrac{\text{cup}}{\text{up}} \; corr}{\text{particle}}}{\dfrac{\text{s/np}}{} >} \quad \dfrac{\dfrac{\text{the}}{\text{np/n}} \; \dfrac{\text{ball}}{\text{n}}}{\text{np}} > \\ \text{s} >$$

Figure 6.4: CCG derivation of "pick cup the ball".

syntactic features — In order to achieve that, we include in the feature vector $\mathbf{f}(x, y)$ a new feature for each non-standard rule, which counts the number of times the rule was applied in the parse.

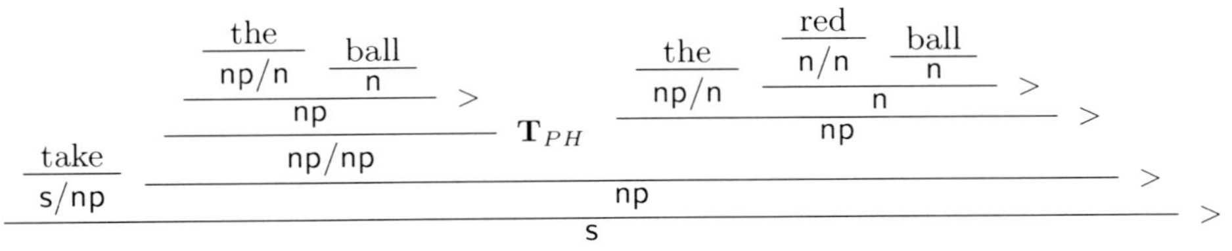

```
                      the      ball                    red    ball
                      ───      ────            the     ───    ────
                      np/n      n              ───     n/n     n
                      ──────────── >           np/n    ─────────── >
          take            np                   ─────       n
          ────   ──────────────── T_PH                 ─────────── >
          s/np         np/np                              np
                 ───────────────────────────────────────────────── >
                                         np
          ─────────────────────────────────────────────────────── >
                                        s
```

Figure 6.5: CCG derivation for the utterance "take the ball the red ball", containing a self-correction.

In the derivation shown in the Figure 6.4, the rule *corr* (correction of a speech recognition error) is applied once, so the corresponding feature value is set to 1. The feature values for the remaining rules are set to 0, since they are absent from the parse. The Figure 6.5 illustrates another example where the rule $\mathbf{T}_{PH}$ is used.

These syntactic features can be seen as a *penalty* given to the parses using these non-standard rules, thereby giving a preference to the "normal" parses over them. This mechanism ensures that the grammar relaxation is only applied "as a last resort" when the usual grammatical analysis fails to provide a full parse. Of course, depending on the relative frequency of occurrence of these rules in the training corpus, some of them will be more strongly penalised than others.

6.4.3 Contextual features

One striking characteristic of spoken dialogue is the importance of *context*. A good understanding the visual and discourse contexts is crucial to resolve potential ambiguities and compute the most likely interpretation(s) of a given utterance.

The feature vector $\mathbf{f}(x, y)$ therefore includes various features related to the context:

contextual features

1. *Activated words*: our dialogue system maintains in its working memory a list of contextually activated words (cfr. [Lison and Kruijff, 2008] and Chapter 5). This list is continuously updated as the dialogue and the environment evolves. For each context-dependent word, we include

contextually activated words

one feature counting the number of times it appears in the utterance string[7].

2. *Expected dialogue moves*: for each possible dialogue move, we include one feature indicating if the dialogue move is consistent with the current discourse model. These features ensure for instance that the dialogue move following a QuestionYN is a Accept, Reject or another question (e.g. for clarification requests), but almost never an Opening.

3. *Expected syntactic categories*: for each atomic syntactic category in the CCG grammar, we include one feature indicating if the category is consistent with the current discourse model[8].

It is worth noting that, since the generated training data does not contain *per se* any contextual annotation, the values for the parameter weights associated with the contextual features are set at a fixed constant value for each activated word.

6.4.4 Speech recognition features

Finally, the feature vector $\mathbf{f}(x, y)$ also includes features related to the *speech recognition*. The ASR module outputs a set of (partial) recognition hypotheses, packed in a word lattice. One example of such structure is given in Figure 6.6.

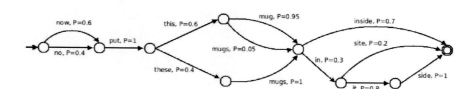

Figure 6.6: Example of a word recognition lattice

Each recognition hypothesis is provided with an associated confidence score, and we want to favour the hypotheses with a high confidence score,

---

[7]Note that this feature is only useful for parsing the *word lattice* produced by the speech recognition- it has obviously no use when parsing a single utterance, since all the parses share the same string.

[8]These features can be used to handle *sentence fragments*, for instance when the full utterance is cut in half by a pause. As an example, imagine a speaker saying "Now give me ...", stopping a few seconds, and then finishing his sentence by "the red ball". In this case, the first part of the utterance waits for an np. When analysing the second part of the utterance, the parses resulting in a np will therefore be preferred.

which are, according to the statistical models incorporated in the ASR, more likely to reflect what was uttered.

To this end, we introduce three features:

1. *Acoustic confidence score*: this feature simply indicates the confidence score given by the ASR module (domain $\in \Re$);

2. *Semantic confidence score*: our ASR system additionally provides a semantic confidence score which we also use for parse selection;

3. *ASR ranking*: finally, we also include information about the hypothesis rank (from best to worst) in the word lattice.

confidence scores

The parameters weights for the three speech recognition features described above are set using regression tests.

6.5 Additional extensions

There are two possible extensions of our approach which are not (yet) implemented in the dialogue system, but are worth describing in some detail. The first one is the integration of the discriminative model into the incremental parser, as a tool for chart scoring (and early update during training). The second extension pertains to the learning algorithm: it might be interesting to see if we can improve our results by replacing the perceptron algorithm with more powerful techniques such as Max-margin classifiers.

6.5.1 Incremental parse selection

The first possible extension of our approach is to make our system *fully incremental*.

Chart scoring

As we explained in section 6.3.3, the decoding algorithm cannot rely directly on dynamic programming techniques, since our features are not strictly local. But we can take advantage of the *incremental* nature of the CCG parser to achieve a similar search space reduction.

Indeed, it is possible to use parse selection not only as a post-parsing step, but also as a **chart scorer** during the incremental parsing. After each incremental step, the parse selection component can be applied to remove the partial parses with a low probability from the chart, thereby ensuring that the size of **GEN**(x) remains bounded.

chart scoring

Type	Feature description
Semantic features	- Occurrences of specific nominals
	- Occurrences of specific ontological sorts
	- Occurrences of specific dependency relations
	- Occurrences of specific sequences (bigrams) of dependency relations
	- Existence of at least one well-formed parse
Syntactic features	- Use of non-standard CCG rules
Contextual features	- Occurrences of contextually activated words
	- Coherence with expected dialogue moves
	- Coherence with expected syntactic categories
Speech recognition features	- Acoustic confidence score
	- Semantic confidence score
	- Rank

Table 6.1: Summary of the features $\mathbf{f}(x, y)$

Collins and Roark [2004] use the following technique to filter the low-probability parses: Let p_k be the kth ranked parse (from best to worst) in $\mathbf{GEN}_i(x)$ - which is the set of possible parses of x at incremental step i. Then p_k will be discarded from the packed chart if $\mathbf{w}^T \cdot \mathbf{f}(x, p_k) < \theta_k$, with the threshold θ_k being defined as

$$\theta_k = \mathbf{w}^T \cdot \mathbf{f}(x, p_0) - \frac{\gamma}{k^3} \qquad (6.13)$$

where γ is a parameter controlling the "strength" of the filtering.

An incremental chart scoring algorithm based on parse selection has been implemented in our cognitive architecture, and is presented in detail in Lison [2009]. Evaluation results on the Wizard-of-Oz test suite notably demonstrate significant improvements in parsing time

Early update during training

The *training* algorithm can also be made incremental. Let (x_i, z_i) be an arbitrary training example, where x_i is an utterance and z_i the expected logical form. And let $y_i^* = \mathrm{argmax}_{y \in \mathbf{GEN}(x_i, z_i)} \mathbf{w}^T \cdot \mathbf{f}(x_i, y)$ denote the best parse which can generate the logical form z_i, i.e. the "gold standard" parse[9].

early update

Once the parse y_i^* is found, we can easily derive a set of *partial parses* from it. We define $y_{i(k)}^*$ to be the "gold standard" partial parse of the training example (x_i, z_i) at step k (i.e when parsing the first k words of utterance x_i).

In [**Algorithm 1**], the parameter update is done by directly applying the decoding algorithm on the full utterance x_i and comparing the selected parse y' to the gold standard parse y^*. The whole update process can be made incremental by a simple modification of the algorithm: instead of parsing the full utterance x_i in one pass, we parse it incrementally, and at each step k we compare the partial parse $y'_{(k)}$ selected according to the current model to the gold standard partial parse $y_{(k)}^*$.

If it appears that these two partial parses do not match, we exit the parsing process for the whole utterance, and perform the parameter update based on the partial parses:

$$\mathbf{w} = \mathbf{w} + \mathbf{f}(x_i, y_{(k)}^*) - \mathbf{f}(x_i, y'_{(k)}) \qquad (6.14)$$

This simple modification has been shown to significantly improve the accuracy of the learning algorithm [Collins and Roark, 2004]. The motivation behind it is very intuitive: when an error in parse selection has been made, it makes sense to correct the parameters *at the point where the error has been*

---

[9]see [**Algorithm 1**] for details.

made rather than on the full parses. It can also increase the efficiency of the algorithm since we do not necessarily have to parse the full utterance for each iteration.

6.5.2 Max-margin classifier (SVM)

Max-margin classifier

Support Vector Machine

We should also consider the use of more sophisticated learning algorithms instead of a simple perceptron. A **Max-margin classifier** – otherwise known as a *Support Vector Machine* [SVM] – could be an interesting solution. Here is how the learning problem should be formulated in our case (see also Collins [2004] for details).

Given parameter values $\mathbf{w}$, the distance between an arbitrary parse y and the correct parse y_i for the ith training example is

$$M_{i,y} = \mathbf{w}^T \cdot \mathbf{f}(x_i, y_i) - \mathbf{w}^T \cdot \mathbf{f}(x_i, y) \tag{6.15}$$

with $y_i = \arg\max_{y \in \mathbf{GEN}(x_i, z_i)} \mathbf{w}^T \cdot \mathbf{f}(x_i, y)$. SVM learning is based on the idea of margin *maximisation*. For a given example (x_i, y_i) and a parameter vector $\mathbf{w}$, the margin is defined as the distance between the first best parse y_i and the second best one:

$$\gamma_\mathbf{w}^i = \frac{1}{||\mathbf{w}||} \left[\mathbf{w}^T \cdot \mathbf{f}(x_i, y_i) - \max_{y \in \mathbf{GEN}(x), y \neq y_i} \mathbf{w}^T \cdot \mathbf{f}(x_i, y) \right] \tag{6.16}$$

The margin therefore represents the normalised distance between the best parse and the "second best parse" for a given utterance.

On the entire training set, the margin $\gamma_\mathbf{w}$ is defined as

$$\gamma_\mathbf{w} = \min_i \gamma_\mathbf{w}^i \tag{6.17}$$

If the data is separable (i.e. there exists at least one $\mathbf{w}$ where $\gamma_\mathbf{w} > 0$), the best classifier is the one which maximises the margin between the "good parse" and the others:

$$\mathbf{w}^* = \operatorname*{argmax}_{\mathbf{w} \in \Re^d} \gamma_\mathbf{w} \tag{6.18}$$

The method involves solving the following constrained optimisation problem in order to determine $\mathbf{w}^*$:

Minimise

$$||\mathbf{w}||^2 - C \sum_{i=1}^n \epsilon_i \tag{6.19}$$

with respect to **w**, ϵ_i for $i = 1...n$
under the constraints

$$\forall i, \forall y \neq y_i, \quad M_{i,y} \geq 1 - \epsilon_i \qquad (6.20)$$
$$\forall i, \quad \epsilon_i \geq 0 \qquad (6.21)$$

where ϵ_i are *slack variables*.

For the perceptron, SVMs, and conditional random fields, the final parameter values can be expressed using the dual variables $\alpha_{i,y}$:

$$\mathbf{w} = \sum_{i=1}^{n} \sum_{y \in \mathbf{GEN}(x)} \alpha_{i,y} \left[\mathbf{f}(x_i, y_i) - \mathbf{f}(x_i, y) \right] \qquad (6.22)$$

In order to train the SVM, the dual variables are set to initial values and then gradually updated on basis of the training examples. The update rule is:

$$\forall i, y, \quad \alpha'_{i,y} = \frac{\alpha_{i,y} e^{\eta \nabla_{i,y}}}{\sum_y \alpha_{i,y} e^{\eta \nabla_{i,y}}} \qquad (6.23)$$

where

- η is the learning rate
- $\nabla_{i,y} = 0$ for $y = y_i$
- $\nabla_{i,y} = 1 - M_{i,y}$ for $y \neq y_i$.

6.6 Summary of the chapter

In this chapter, we detailed our approach to *robust parsing of spoken inputs*. We first gave a short overview of the state-of-the-art techniques used in this domain. These can be classified in three groups: shallow parsing techniques, pure statistical approaches, and controlled relaxation. Our approach belongs to the latter set of techniques. It relies on a *grammar relaxation* mechanism coupled with a *discriminative model* selecting the most appropriate interpretations, according to a set of linguistic and contextual features.

In the first section, we explained how the grammar relaxation mechanism precisely works. Four groups of *non-standard rules* have been added to the CCG parser: new type-shifting rules, paradigmatic heap rules, discourse-level composition rules, and ASR correction rules.

We then detailed the formal properties of the *discriminative model* used for parse selection. Based on a parameter vector, the model assigns a *score* to each interpretation according to the value of its features. The interpretation with the highest score is then selected. We outlined the learning algorithm (an *averaged perceptron*), the training data on which it operates, and discussed some technicalities regarding the decoding operation.

We presented the various linguistic and contextual features which have been integrated into our discriminative model. They are of four different sorts: *semantic features* (defined on the substructures of the logical form); *syntactic features* (defined on the derivational history of the parse); *contextual features* (defined on the situated and dialogue contexts), and finally *speech recognition features* (defined on ASR scores).

In the last section, we discussed two possible extensions of our approach, one pertaining to the *incrementality* of the parsing process (how can we use the discriminative model *during* parsing to prune unlikely interpretations), and the other pertaining to the *learning algorithm* (how can we replace the perceptron by a max-margin classifier).

In the next chapter, we present the experimental results of our approach.

Part III

Evaluation & Conclusion

7
Evaluation

This chapter presents the evaluation results of our approach to robust processing of spoken dialogue. We start by describing the testing data, collected during Wizard-of-Oz experiments. We then present the evaluation procedure, explain the type of quantitative results we extracted (exact-match, partial-match and word error rate), give detailed figures for each of them, and close the chapter by a discussion of the results.

7.1 Testing data

The test suite is composed of 195 individual utterances collected during **Wizard-of-Oz experiments**[1]. These experiments consist of a set of situated human-robot interactions relative to a shared visual scene. A total of seven such experiments were conducted, all with members of the CoSy research team. The interactions were free both in form and content – they could include questions, assertions, commands, answers or clarifications. The only imposed constraint was to interact with the robot about the visual scene (and nothing else). All the interactions were done in English[2].

Wizard-of-Oz experiments

The scene included objects of various sizes, shapes and colors. The robot (simulated by a human being) was able to recognise these objects, talk about their properties, ask questions regarding what it did not know, and grasp/move the objects within the scene.

All these interactions were recorded with a headset microphone. The audio data resulting from these experiments were subsequently *segmented*

---

[1]These 195 utterances are distinct from the 250 utterances used for the experiments regarding situated speech recognition (cfr. Chapter 5).

[2]It should be noted that six out of the seven interactions were conducted with non-native English speakers, hence complicating the task of speech recognition.

utterance-by-utterance. Each speech segment was then manually *transcribed*, and *associated with a semantic annotation* (its "gold standard" logical form). The semantic annotation was realised semi-automatically, using the domain-specific grammar described in Appendix C to provide an initial annotation, which was then manually corrected.

7.2 Evaluation procedure

Once the preparation of the testing data was complete, we started the evaluation procedure, which followed these steps (illustrated in Figure 7.1):

1. The audio data corresponding to each utterance is sent to the dialogue comprehension system.

2. The speech recogniser computes a set of *recognition hypotheses* ("NBests") and sends the resulting *word lattice* to the incremental parser;

3. The incremental parser takes the *word lattice* as input, parses it, and outputs a *packed logical form*;

4. The discriminative model is then applied to the packed logical form, and assigns a *score* to each interpretation;

5. The interpretation with the highest score is selected, and is *compared* to the desired interpretation (i.e. the one manually specified in the semantic annotation for the utterance).

6. *Three quantitative results* are then extracted from this comparison: exact-match, partial-match, and word error rate.

7. The above procedure is repeated for each utterance included in the test suite.

7.3 Types of quantitative results

Three types of quantitative results are extracted from the evaluation output (see also Collins [2003] for more details on possible measures):

exact-match

1. **Exact-match**: does the selected logical form match *exactly* the expected "gold standard" logical form? By "exactly", we mean that

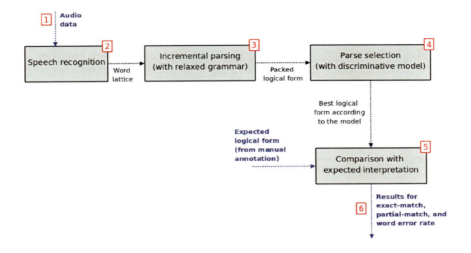

Figure 7.1: Simplified evaluation workflow

there must exist a *one-to-one* relation between each substructure[3] of the logical forms (modulo variable renaming). If the match is perfect, the exact-match result for this utterance is set to 1, and 0 otherwise.

2. **Partial-match**: how many *substructures* of the chosen logical form are matching *substructures* of the expected logical form? To get the partial-match result for the utterance, we count the number of substructure matches, and then divide the result by the total number of substructures in the logical form.

partial-match

3. **Word error rate**: we compare the phonological string which produced the interpretation to the *original* utterance from the transcript (i.e. without speech recognition errors), and derive the word error rate from it. The word error rate is defined as:

Word error rate

$$WER = \frac{S + D + I}{N} \quad (7.1)$$

where S is the number of substitutions, D is the number of the deletions, I is the number of the insertions, and N is the total number of words in the original utterance.

---

[3]The substructures of a logical form are defined to be either (1) a nominal, (2) a dependency relation between nominals, or (3) a feature included in a nominal.

For the exact- and partial-match results, we give the precision, recall, and F_1-measure. Their values are defined in terms of true positives (TP), false positives (FP) and false negatives (FN). For our task, these are simple counts:

$$\text{TP} = \#\text{utterances correctly matched} \tag{7.2}$$

$$\text{FP} = \#\text{utterances incorrectly matched} \tag{7.3}$$

$$\text{FN} = \#\text{utterances with no computed interpretation} \tag{7.4}$$

The precision, recall and F_1 measure are then computed on these counts:

$$\text{precision} = \frac{\text{TP}}{\text{TP} + \text{FP}} \tag{7.5}$$

$$\text{recall} = \frac{\text{TP}}{\text{TP} + \text{FN}} \tag{7.6}$$

$$F_1 = 2 \times \frac{(\text{precision} \times \text{recall})}{\text{precision} + \text{recall}} \tag{7.7}$$

7.4 Quantitative results

The Tables 7.1, 7.2 and 7.3 present our quantitative results. These tables only show the most important values, see Appendix B for all details.

We ran the entire test suite over each possible combination of activated features and grammar relaxation, and repeated the operation for NBest 1, 3, 5, and 10. Only NBest 1 and 5 are shown in the tables 7.1 and 7.2.

Each line shown in the tables corresponds to a possible configuration. For each configuration, we analyse the accuracy results on different NBests, and give the precision, recall and F_1 value for each.

The first cell of the first line corresponds to the baseline: no grammar relaxation, no activated features, and use of the first NBest recognition hypothesis. The last line corresponds to the final results with all features, combined with the grammar relaxation mechanism.

Two elements are worth noticing in these results:

1. In each of the three tables, we observe that no configuration is able to beat the results obtained with all activated features. In other words, it shows that all features types are playing a positive role on the task, they all "play their part".

2. Likewise, we observe that taking into account more ASR recognition hypotheses has a positive effect on the results: the results obtained using ten recognition hypotheses are substantially better than those obtained based only on the first hypothesis.

7.4.1 Comparison with baseline

Here are the comparative results we obtained:

- Regarding the exact-match accuracy results, the difference between the baseline results and the results with our approach (grammar relaxation and all features activated for NBest 5) is striking: the F_1-measure climbs from 43.0 % to 66.9 %, which means a relative difference of **55.6 %**.

- For the partial-match, the F_1-measure goes from 68.0 % for the baseline to 86.8 % for our approach – a relative increase of **27.6 %**.

- Finally, the decrease in Word Error Rate is also worth noting: we go from 20.5 % for the baseline to 15.7 % with our approach. The difference is statistically significant (p-value for t-tests is 0.036), and the relative decrease is of **23.4 %**.

Gram. Relax.	Activated Features				Nbest 1			Nbest 5		
	Sem.	Synt.	Ac.	Cont.	Pr.	R.	F_1	Pr.	R.	F_1
					40.9	45.2	**43.0**	14.4	13.9	14.2
				×	35.2	41.5	38.1	28.8	31.8	30.2
			×		42.8	46.3	44.5	38.1	47.1	42.2
			×	×	41.9	45.8	43.7	43.1	49.4	46.0
		×			59.0	54.3	56.6	30.3	51.3	38.1
		×		×	59.0	54.3	56.6	35.2	55.1	43.0
		×	×		59.0	54.3	56.6	58.3	65.4	61.6
		×	×	×	59.0	54.3	56.6	60.8	66.3	63.4
×					20.9	49.0	29.3	10.7	34.1	16.3
×				×	20.9	49.0	29.3	12.1	39.0	18.4
×			×		27.1	55.5	36.4	27.3	54.6	36.4
×			×	×	21.7	50.0	30.2	27.9	56.2	37.3
×		×			34.1	61.1	43.7	21.0	39.6	27.4
×		×		×	30.2	58.2	39.7	21.9	44.2	29.3
×		×	×		34.1	61.1	43.7	32.8	59.1	42.2
×		×	×	×	32.5	60.0	42.2	32.5	60.0	42.2
×	×				49.6	69.5	57.9	28.9	77.7	42.2
×	×			×	49.6	69.5	57.9	31.0	78.9	44.5
×	×		×		49.6	69.5	57.9	52.1	83.1	64.0
×	×		×	×	49.6	69.5	57.9	53.1	84.4	65.2
×	×	×			52.7	70.8	60.4	29.6	78.1	43.0
×	×	×		×	52.7	70.8	60.4	31.7	79.3	45.3
×	×	×	×		52.7	70.8	60.4	54.6	82.7	65.8
×	×	×	×	×	52.7	70.8	**60.4**	55.6	84.0	**66.9**

Table 7.1: Exact-match accuracy results, broken down by activated features, use of grammar relaxation, and number of recognition hypotheses considered. For each configuration, we give the precision, recall, and F_1 value. This is a reduced table, see Table B.1 for details.

Gram. Relax.	Activated Features				Nbest 1			Nbest 5		
	Sem.	Synt.	Ac.	Cont.	Pr.	R.	F_1	Pr.	R.	F_1
					86.2	56.2	**68.0**	73.5	45.8	56.4
				×	85.5	56.0	67.7	81.3	54.2	65.1
			×		86.8	56.4	68.3	84.3	60.4	70.4
			×	×	86.2	56.2	68.1	85.4	60.4	70.7
		×			90.5	57.4	70.3	80.1	66.4	72.6
		×		×	90.5	57.4	70.3	83.3	67.2	74.4
		×	×		90.5	57.4	70.3	88.9	67.1	76.4
		×	×	×	90.5	57.4	70.3	89.5	67.2	76.8
×					75.7	73.3	74.5	71.4	81.9	76.3
×				×	73.7	72.8	73.2	71.7	78.7	75.1
×			×		75.3	73.2	74.2	74.6	73.1	73.8
×			×	×	72.7	72.5	72.6	74.6	74.1	74.4
×		×			80.9	74.6	77.6	76.2	72.1	74.1
×		×		×	80.2	74.4	77.2	78.7	76.2	77.4
×		×	×		80.8	74.6	77.6	80.3	74.5	77.3
×		×	×	×	80.4	74.5	77.3	80.3	75.5	77.8
×	×				86.5	75.8	80.8	80.7	88.4	84.4
×	×			×	86.5	75.8	80.8	80.0	88.3	84.0
×	×		×		86.5	75.8	80.8	86.2	86.7	86.4
×	×		×	×	86.5	75.8	80.8	86.3	87.2	86.8
×	×	×			88.1	76.2	81.7	79.3	88.2	83.5
×	×	×		×	88.1	76.2	81.7	81.7	88.5	85.0
×	×	×	×		88.1	76.2	81.7	87.5	85.4	86.4
×	×	×	×	×	88.1	76.2	**81.7**	87.6	86.0	**86.8**

Table 7.2: Partial-match accuracy results, broken down by activated features, use of grammar relaxation, and number of recognition hypotheses considered. For each configuration, we give the precision, recall, and F_1 value. This is a reduced table, see Table B.2 for details.

Gram. Relax.	Activated Features				Nbest 1	Nbest 3	Nbest 5	Nbest 10
	Sem.	Synt.	Ac.	Cont.				
					20.5	26.9	29.7	25.9
				×	20.5	23.6	24.6	28.0
			×		20.5	19.7	19.6	19.7
			×	×	20.5	18.7	18.2	18.3
	×				20.5	24.6	25.6	31.2
	×			×	20.5	21.4	23.2	26.1
	×		×		20.5	18.3	18.4	18.1
	×		×	×	20.5	17.3	17.4	17.4
×					19.6	23.6	25.9	23.9
×				×	19.3	20.4	23.3	26.7
×			×		19.7	18.6	18.4	19.3
×			×	×	19.4	18.0	17.6	17.7
×		×			19.4	24.6	26.9	27.9
×		×		×	19.4	22.2	23.9	28.1
×		×	×		19.4	18.8	18.7	18.8
×		×	×	×	19.4	17.8	17.3	17.4
×	×				20.2	22.4	25.5	29.4
×	×			×	20.2	21.0	22.9	26.1
×	×		×		20.2	17.8	17.8	17.8
×	×		×	×	20.2	17.4	17.1	17.1
×	×	×			19.4	21.5	24.3	28.7
×	×	×		×	19.4	19.8	21.9	25.9
×	×	×	×		19.4	16.8	16.7	16.7
×	×	×	×	×	19.4	16.5	15.7	15.7

Table 7.3: Word Error Rate results, broken down by activated features, use of grammar relaxation, and number of recognition hypotheses considered. For each configuration, we give the word error rate, in percents. This is a reduced table, see Table B.3 for details.

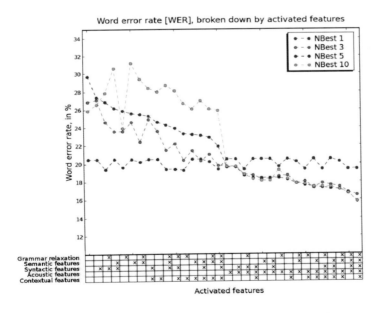

Figure 7.2: Word error rate, broken down by activated features (graphical illustration of Table 7.3).

7.5 Discussion of results

The analysis of the parse selection output is interesting in many respects. Here are a few lessons we learned from our evaluation:

- The first lesson we learned is the importance of *tuning the ASR system correctly*[4]. The initial results we obtained for our approach were done with a non-optimised ASR system, yielding a word error rate of over 30 %. When we applied our robust parsing system to this data set, we realised that the comparative results were far below our expectations.

  Upon analysing the output in detail, it appeared that the primary reason was the very low accuracy of the ASR recognition hypotheses. In many cases, the recognition hypotheses were completely "off the mark" compared to what was uttered. As a result, the parse selection module could not function properly because the given input was too noisy to be of any practical use.

  The grammar relaxation mechanism and the discriminative model can only be effective if, for a given utterance, its "gold standard" transcription and its actual recognition hypotheses bear at least some resemblance with each other. If the word lattice input contains only non-sensical data, we should not be surprised to see the robust parsing system fail to provide a sensical interpretation. As the famous computer science axiom says: "Garbage In, Garbage Out".

- The second, related lesson we can derive from our evaluation is that, in practical spoken dialogue systems, *speech recognition errors largely outweight all other issues* (ill-formed inputs, syntactic ambiguities, etc.). The non-standard rules which proved to be most useful were – by far – the ASR correction rules. The type-shifting rules turned out to be only marginally useful, not because the spoken language phenomena they sought to handle were absent from the testing data (to the contrary), but because they were overshadowed by the pervasiveness of speech recognition errors.

- While experimenting with our robust parsing model, we realised that the correct calibration of the grammar relaxation mechanism was absolutely crucial to maintain a reasonable computational efficiency. Some of the non-standard combinatory rules we introduced (such as the

---

[4]ASR software such as Nuance usually come with a large set of technical parameters which have to be tuned, such as the relative weights of the acoustic and language models, pruning thresholds, activation of noise cancellation, etc.

"paradigmatic heap" rules) turned out to be "overkill" on our evaluation test suite: they significantly slowed down processing (due to a large increase in the search space) while contributing minimally to the interpretation. Most of the type-shifting rules and paradigmatic heap rules were therefore deactivated when computationally expensive experiments had to be performed.

- Most importantly, the evaluation results demonstrate the *adequacy of our approach to robust parsing*. In the introductory chapter, we outlined three essential characteristics of our approach. Let us recapitulate them briefly, and compare our design choices to the experimental results we obtained:

    1. Our system is based on a *hybrid* symbolic/statistical approach, combining a grammar relaxation mechanism to a statistical discriminative model. As the evaluation results show, this strategy turned out to be highly successful: we are able to achieve very significant increases in both *precision* and *recall*, while retaining a *deep, fined-grained* linguistic analysis.

    2. The second defining characteristic of our approach is its high level of *integration*. Here again, the results speak for themselves: we observe that all the features (semantic, syntactic, acoustic or contextual) play a positive role in discriminating the correct interpretations from the incorrect ones. And the highest result is achieved when all these features are activated.

    3. Finally, we designed our system to be *context-sensitive*. And this strategy also turned out to be a fruitful one. Contextual knowledge is able to significantly improve the accuracy of our results, by filtering out the ASR recognition hypotheses which are contextually unlikely.

8
Conclusion

This chapter concludes our thesis. We first present a brief summary of what we have achieved, stepping back from the implementation details to see the bigger picture. We recapitulate the issues we tried to address, the approach we developed to this end, and the experimental results we obtained. We then provide suggestions for further research.

In the introductory chapter, we detailed four important issues hampering the development of robust systems for spoken dialogue comprehension. Let us briefly recapitulate what these issues were. The first issue is the difficulty of accommodating *spoken language phenomena* (disfluencies, sentence fragments, elided or ungrammatical utterances, etc.) in the system. A second problem facing dialogue systems is the pervasiveness of *speech recognition errors*, speech recognition being a highly error-prone task, particularly for open-ended discourse domains. And finally, dialogue systems must also find ways to handle the *ambiguities* arising at all processing levels, and the various *extra-grammatical* constructions encountered.

This thesis presented an original approach to address these complex issues in the context of domain-specific dialogues for human-robot interaction [HRI]. Our implementation is fully integrated in a *cognitive architecture* for "talking robots" – that is, robots which are able to interact socially with humans using spoken dialogue to achieve a range of service-related tasks. The cognitive architecture is composed of a number of cooperating subsystems for vision, motor control, navigation, planning, and of course communication. The various components we developed to make spoken dialogue comprehension more robust are all part of the *communication subsystem*, and span multiple processing levels, from the initial speech signal up to the semantic and pragmatic interpretation.

The approach advocated here is strongly inspired by recent experimental findings in psycholinguistics and cognitive science regarding *situated human language processing*. Contextual knowledge is used at every step to guide the interpretation process, either to *anticipate* what is going to be said (this is realised via e.g. the context sensitive language models described in Chapter 5), or to *discriminate* between the possible interpretations of a given utterance (cfr. the robust parsing model described in Chapter 6).

A *hybrid symbolic/statistical processing strategy* is used for parsing the word lattices. It combines fine-grained linguistic resources (the CCG grammar) with automatically trained statistical models. This way, we are able to achieve both *deep* and *robust* spoken dialogue processing.

Practically, robust parsing is realised via a *controlled relaxation* of the grammatical constraints. A set of non-standard combinatory rules are introduced in the grammar to this end. The role of such non-standard rules is to account for various spoken language phenomena (missing words, "paradigmatic heaps", discourse-level compositions) and correct possible speech recognition errors.

At the end of the "relaxed" parsing operation, a (potentially large) set of semantic interpretations is outputted by the CCG parser. In order to select the most likely interpretation, a discriminative model is applied. The discriminative model assigns a *score* to each interpretation. A decoding algorithm is responsible for computing these scores. It works as follows. First, the algorithm extracts a set of linguistic and contextual features relative to the parse, and records the corresponding values in a *feature vector*. This feature vector is then projected against a perceptron-trained parameter vector, and the *linear combination* of the feature vector and the parameter vector gives the final score for the interpretation.

One of the biggest advantage of *discriminative* models is the possibility to integrate virtually *any* kind of feature which might be useful – without being tied (as for generative models) to the particular variables being generated by the model. A wide range of features are included in our approach. They are extracted from the semantic, syntactic, acoustic and contextual representations. Others features could be easily incorporated in the future.

We performed an extensive empirical evaluation of our work. The evaluation results on a "Wizard of Oz" test suite demonstrated very significant improvements both in *accuracy* and *robustness*, with notably a **55.6** % increase in the exact-match accuracy of the final chosen interpretation over the baseline performance. Partial-match accuracy is similarly improved (increase of **27.6** % compared to the baseline). Word error rate decreases from **20.5** % for the baseline to **15.7** % with our model.

8.1 Suggestions for further research

The approach presented in this thesis can be improved and extended in many possible ways.

Enhancing the *speech recognition* component is probably the single extension which would bring the most significant improvements in terms of empirical results. As we explained during the discussion of results in the evaluation chapter, the speech recognition errors indeed currently largely outweight all other issues. Several lines of work can be envisioned.

1. The first one, which is purely technical but not to be neglected, would consist of technological improvements regarding the ASR software, the incorporated acoustic models, and the use of a microphone array instead of a simple microphone.

2. The use of more sophisticated (and trained on a larger and more varied set of training data) language models is also expected to significantly improve the speech recognition performance.

3. The salience-based models of context we developed are currently quite simple. A more sophisticated statistical modeling of the situated and discourse context would be interesting, and could possibly lead to better results [Wiggers, 2008].

The robust parsing component also provides room for multiple interesting extensions. We already outlined two of these extensions at the end of Chapter 6.

4. The first extension concerns the exploitation of the discriminative model *during* incremental parsing, as a tool for chart scoring. As we explained, this extension could also be fruitfully used within the learning loop, to improve the perceptron training.

5. The second possible improvement is related to the algorithm used for parameter estimation. We believe it might be worth considering the use of more sophisticated learning algorithms such as max-margin classifiers, instead of a simple perceptron.

6. There are still other aspects of the learning process which might be improved. The search space in which the perceptron operates is currently rather limited. As we have explained in the previous chapters, some parameter weights in the discriminative model (those for the contextual

and speech recognition features) are set manually or using regression tests, instead of being automatically learned. The ASR correction rules are also specified manually, by analysing the most frequent sources of errors.

Investigating how these operations could be automatised while avoiding data sparsity problems or an explosion of the search space would certainly constitute an interesting line of future research.

7. Regarding the grammar relaxation, a more precise specification of the "paradigmatic heap" rules would surely be beneficial to the grammatical coverage of our system. In particular, an explicit distinction should be made between the heaps which incorporate the semantics of each of their elements (such as for enumerations), and the heaps which should only retain the last element and discard the others (such as for repetitions and corrections).

8. On a more technical level, another possible improvement concerns the parsing algorithm. As we explained in the previous chapter, our CCG parser takes *word lattices* as input, and analyse them in an incremental fashion. The current algorithm that we developed is however not optimal. Several efficient algorithms for parsing word lattices are described in the literature [Tomita, 1986; Staab, 1995], but, to the best of our knowledge, none are fully incremental. Devising a new, more efficient algorithm for incremental CCG parsing of word lattices would constitute an interesting forthcoming work.

9. The parse selection mechanism (implemented via our discriminative model) currently works on full interpretations. The controlled relaxation techniques allow us to extract interpretations in many cases of ill-formed or extra-grammatical utterances, but it can still remain insufficient. One possible solution would be to expand our approach to *partial* parse selection [Zhang et al., 2007]. Some kind of *island parsing* mechanism would then be necessary to extract partial analyses. As our grammatical analysis is based on Combinatory Categorial Grammar, such a mechanism is perfectly possible and can be realised efficiently. An interesting question to address in this case is how to combine *island parsing* with *incrementality*.

10. Finally, the current approach is limited to domain-specific dialogues, for which developing a full-scale symbolic grammar by hand is conceivable. It would be interesting to investigate the potential extension of our

approach to handle *generic*, domain-independent dialogues, which are not limited to a particular task, domain or vocabulary.

This would probably require the use of lexical acquisition techniques (see e.g. Cholakov *et al.* [2008]; Zettlemoyer and Collins [2007]), as well as of broad-coverage statistical models [Collins, 1997; Charniak, 2001; He and Young, 2005; Clark and Curran, 2007].

The biggest advantage of such an extension would be the possibility to directly compare the performance of our model with other approaches based on *standardised benchmarks*, such as the ATIS corpus of spoken dialogue [Dahl *et al.*, 1994].

Part IV

Appendices

Packing algorithm

A *packing* mechanism [Oepen and Carroll, 2000; Carroll and Oepen, 2005] is used by the incremental parser to efficiently represent and manipulate logical forms across the communication subarchitecture. A packed logical form [PLF] represents content similar across the different analyses of a given input as a single graph, using over- and underspecification of how different nodes can be connected to capture lexical and syntactic forms of ambiguity.

After each incremental step, the resulting set of logical forms is compacted into a single representation, which can then be directly manipulated by various processes, in order, for example, to prune unsupported interpretations. It can also be *unpacked*, i.e. the original logical forms can be completely regenerated (this is done by *traversing* the packed structure).

The packed representations are made of two basic elements: *packing nodes* and *packing edges*. A packing node groups a set of nominals sharing identical properties and named relations under a particular subset of the logical forms. Packing edges are responsible for connecting the different packing nodes together, thus ensuring the correspondence between the packed structure and the set of logical forms it represents.

The packing of logical forms is performed in two main steps:

1. An initial PLF is first constructed on the basis of the set of logical forms (*Step 1* of Algorithm 2). To this end, each logical form is traversed and its nominals are used to populate the packed structure.

2. The resulting structure is then compacted by merging particular substructures (*Step 2* of Algorithm 2).

A.1 Example

The Figures A.1-A.3 below exemplify a simple case of packing operation. The parsed utterance is "Take the ball to the left of the box". Two distinct readings can be derived, depending on the interpretation of the phrase "to the left of the box". In the first reading (LF_1 in the figure A.1), the robot is asked to take the ball and put it to the left of the box - the phrase is thus seen as indicating the *direction* of the move. In the second reading (LF_2) however, "to the left of the box" indicates the *location* of the ball to take.

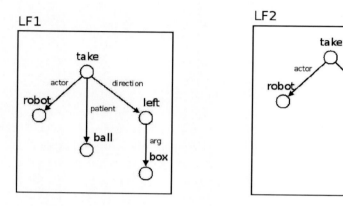

Figure A.1: The two initial logical forms LF_1 and LF_2 retrieved from parsing the utterance "Take the ball to the left of the box"

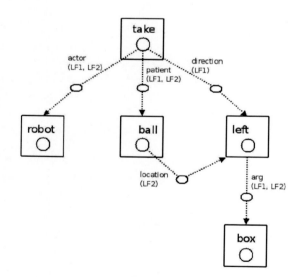

Figure A.2: The resulting packed logical form, before compacting

Figure A.2 illustrates the application of the first step of the packing operation. A packing node - drawn in the figure as a square - is created for each nominal. A packing edge is constituted for each relation found in the logical forms. As shown in the figure, some packing edges are shared by both logical forms, whereas others are only evidenced in one of them. An example of the first case is the edge between "take" and "robot", which shared by the two logical forms LF_1 and LF_2. The edge between "take" and "left" illustrates the second case: it is only evidenced in LF_1.

In the example we present here, all packing edges have only one packing node target. In the general case however, several distinct targets can be specified within the same edge.

During the second step, the packed structure is compacted by merging packing nodes. The criteria to decide whether two packing nodes can be merged is the following: if (1) two packing nodes are connected by a packing edge, and if (2) the logical form identifiers for the head node, the edge and the target node are all identical, then the two packing nodes can be merged. For example, the packing node surrounding "take" and the one surrounding "robot" can be merged, since the two nodes and the edge between them are present both in LF_1 and LF_2.

The compacting operation is repeated until no more merges are possible. In our case, illustrated in the figure A.3, we are left with two packing nodes, one rooted on the nominal "take", and one on "left".

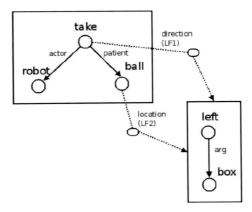

Figure A.3: The final packed logical form, after compacting

A.2 Data structures

We present below the informal specifications of the various data structures used to construct PLFs. See figure A.5 for a graphical representation.

PackedLogicalForm:
- id: packed logical form identifier
- packingNodes: set of packing nodes
- root: root packing node

PackingNode:
- id: packing node identifier
- packedNominals: set of packed nominals
- lfIds: set of LF identifiers, enumerating the logical forms in which the nominals included in the packing node are present
- root: root nominal

PackedNominal:
- id: packed nominal identifier
- sort: ontological sort
- prop: logical proposition
- features: set of packed features
- relations: set of internal relations
- packingEdges: set of outgoing packing edges

PackedFeature:
- feature: name of the feature
- value: value of the feature
- lfIds: set of the LF identifiers, enumerating the logical forms in which the feature holds

PackingEdge:
- id: packing edge identifier
- head: head nominal
- mode: edge label
- packingNodeTargets: set of packing node targets

PackingNodeTarget:
- lfIds: set of LF identifiers, enumerating the logical forms in which the edge exists
- target: packing node targeted by the edge

Figure A.4: Data structures used to construct PLFs

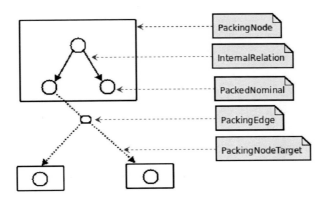

Figure A.5: Graphical representation of the data structures

A.3 Pseudo-code

We finally describe the details of the algorithms used in the packing mechanism we implemented.

Algorithm 2 : `Pack(LFs)` - Packing of a set of logical forms

Require: LFs is a set of logical forms (describing the same utterance)

   % Step 0: Initialization
   rootNominal ← ⟨ rootSort, 'root', ∅, ∅, ∅⟩
   rootNode ← ⟨ {rootNominal}, ∅, rootNominal ⟩
   packingNodes ← {rootNode}
   PLF ← ⟨ packingNodes, rootNode ⟩

   % Step 1: Construction of the packed logical form
   for lf ∈ LFs **do**
      AddLFInformation(lf, PLF)
   end for

   % Step 2: Merge of the packed logical form
   PLF = MergePackedLogicalForm(PLF)

   return PLF

Algorithm 3 : `CreateNewNode(nom)` - using the information in `nom`, create (1) a new packing node, (2) a new packed nominal inside it and (3) new packing edges connected to the latter.

Require: A well-formed nominal nom

   newEdges ← ∅
   for every relation rel in rels(nom) **do**
      % A packing edge is defined with a head nominal, a mode ("edge label"), a set of packing node targets, and a set of logical form identifiers
      newEdge ← ⟨ head(rel), mode(rel), {target(rel)}, {lfId(nom)}⟩,
      newEdges ← newPackingEdges ∪ {newEdge}
   end for

   % A packing nominal comprises an ontological sort, a logical proposition, a set of features, a set of internal relations, and a set of outgoing packing edges
   newNom ← ⟨ sort(nom), prop(nom), feats(nom), ∅, newEdges ⟩

   % A packing node is a triple comprising a set of packing nominals, a set of LF identifiers, and a reference to the root nominal
   newPackingNode ← ⟨{newNom},{lfId(nom)}, newNom⟩

   return newPackingNode

Algorithm 4 : AddLFInformation(lf, PLF) - Add the information contained in lf to the packed logical form.

Require: lf is a well-formed logical form

    for every nominal nom in nominals(lf) **do**

        if there is no packing node in PLF which encapsulates a packed nominal with the ontological sort sort(nom) and the logical proposition prop(nom) **then**

            % *We create a new packing node and its related substructures*
newPackingNode ← CreateNewPackingNode(nom)

            % *We add the packing node to the PLF structure*
packingNodes(PLF) ← packingNodes(PLF) ∪ {newPackingNode}

        else
            % *We update the existing nominal and its dependent edges*
let pNom = the packed nominal with sort(nom) and prop(nom)
let pNode = the packing node encapsulating pNom

            pNode ← IntegrateNominalToPackingNode(nom, pNode)
        end if

        if nom is the root nominal in lf **then**
            % *We establish a connection between the root node and the current one*

            let packingNode = the packing node which encapsulates nom in PLF

            Add a packing edge between root(PLF) and packingNode
lfIds(root(PLF)) = lfIds(root(PLF)) ∪ {id(lf)}
        end if

    end for

    return PLF

Algorithm 5 : IntegrateNominalToPackingNode(nom, pNode) - integrate the information contained in nom to the existing packing node pNode

Require: A well-formed nominal nom
Require: A well formed packing node pNode which already encapsulates a nominal with the same ontological sort and logical proposition as nom

  let pNom = the nominal encapsulated in pNode

  for every relation rel in rels(nom) do
    if ∃ edge ∈ edges(pNom) where mode(rel) = mode(edge) then
      % If there is already a packing edge with same mode, add one packing node target and the LF identifier
      targets(edge)←targets(edge) ∪ {target(rel)}
      lfIds(edge) ← lfIds(edge) ∪ {lfId(nom)}
    else
      % Else, we create a new packing edge
      newEdge ← ⟨ head(rel), mode(rel), {target(rel)}, {lfId(nom)}⟩
      edges(pNom) ← edges(pNom) ∪ {newEdge}
    end if
  end for

  % Update the features in the nominal, and the LF identifiers in the packing node
  feats(pNom) ← feats(pNom) ∪ {feats(nom)}
  lfIds(pNode) ← lfIds(pNode) ∪ {lfId(nom)}

  return pNode

Algorithm 6 : MergePackedLogicalForm(PLF) - compact the PLF representation by merging nominals

Require: PLF a well formed packed logical form

  while there are packing nodes in PLF which can be merged do
    for every packing node packingNode ∈ PLF do
      for every nominal nom ∈ nominals(packingNode) do
        for every edge edge ∈ edges(nom) do
          if edge has only one packing node target then

            let LFS_{head} = set of logical forms identifiers in packingNode
            let LFS_{edge} = set of logical forms identifiers in edge
            let LFS_{target} = set of logical forms identifiers in target(edge)

            if $LFS_{head} = LFS_{edge} = LFS_{target}$ then
              % If the set of logical forms shared by the two packing nodes (and the packing edge between them) is identical, then they can be merged in one packing node

              let targetNom = the head nominal of target(edge)

              Merge packingNode and targetNom into a single packing node

              Transform edge into an internal relation (in the merged packing node) between nom and targetNom

            end if
          end if
        end for
      end for
    end for
  end while
  return PLF

B
Detailed results for parse selection

We present here the detailed quantitative results we obtained regarding the *robust parsing of spoken inputs* using a discriminative model. As we explained in Chapter 7, the test suite is composed of 195 individual utterances collected during Wizard-of-Oz experiments. The evaluation procedure is explained in detail in sections 7.2 and 7.3.

B.1 Tables

For the detailed results shown in the tables B.1, B.2 and B.3, we ran the entire test suite over each possible combination of activated features and grammar relaxation, and repeated the operation for NBest 1, 3, 5, and 10.

Since we have 4 different types of features, plus the possible activation of grammar relaxation rules, the number of possible feature configurations is equal to $\sum_{k=0}^{5} \frac{5!}{k!(5-k)!} = 32$.

Each line shown in the tables corresponds to a possible configuration. For each configuration, we analyse the accuracy results on NBest 1, 3, 5 and 10, and give the precision, recall and F_1 value for each.

The NBest 1 results of the first line correspond to the baseline: no grammar relaxation, no activated features, and use of the first NBest recognition hypothesis. The last line corresponds to the final results with all features, combined with the grammar relaxation mechanism.

Two elements are worth noticing in these detailed results:

1. In each of the three tables, we observe that no configuration is able to improve on the results obtained with all activated features. In other words, it shows that all features types play a positive role on the task.

2. Likewise, we observe that taking into account more ASR recognition hypotheses has a positive effect on the results: the results obtained using ten recognition hypotheses are substantially better than those obtained based only on the first hypothesis.

Table B.1: Exact-match accuracy results, broken down by activated features, use of grammar relaxation, and number of recognition hypotheses considered. For each configuration, we give the precision, recall, and F_1 value (all in percents).

Grammar Relaxation	Activated Features				Nbest 1			Nbest 3			Nbest 5			Nbest 10		
	Semantic	Syntactic	Acoustic	Contextual	Pr.	R.	F_1	Pr.	R.	F_1	Pr.	R.	F_1	Pr.	R.	F_1
					40.9	45.2	**43.0**	23.4	28.0	25.5	14.4	13.9	14.2	22.0	40.0	28.4
				×	35.2	41.5	38.1	31.0	35.2	32.9	28.8	31.8	30.2	25.2	32.5	28.4
			×		42.8	46.3	44.5	41.8	49.4	45.3	38.1	47.1	42.2	43.6	50.5	46.8
			×	×	41.9	45.8	43.7	37.6	46.0	41.4	43.1	49.4	46.0	39.4	47.2	43.0
		×			40.9	45.2	43.0	19.0	25.0	21.5	24.0	29.6	26.5	21.8	33.8	26.5
		×		×	40.9	45.2	43.0	29.1	35.7	32.0	26.2	30.9	28.4	21.8	25.6	23.5
		×	×		43.8	46.9	45.3	38.1	47.1	42.2	40.0	48.3	43.7	41.8	49.4	45.3
		×	×	×	45.7	48.0	46.8	39.4	47.2	43.0	44.0	50.0	46.8	40.3	47.8	43.7
	×				59.0	54.3	56.6	33.6	51.2	40.6	30.3	51.3	38.1	16.6	40.3	23.5
	×			×	59.0	54.3	56.6	42.8	57.3	49.0	35.2	55.1	43.0	26.1	51.5	34.7
	×		×		59.0	54.3	56.6	60.1	64.5	62.2	58.3	65.4	61.6	57.3	66.6	61.6
	×		×	×	59.0	54.3	56.6	61.8	65.1	63.4	60.8	66.3	63.4	59.8	67.5	63.4
	×	×			59.0	54.3	56.6	35.2	52.5	42.2	30.3	51.3	38.1	19.8	44.6	27.4
	×	×		×	59.0	54.3	56.6	43.6	57.7	49.7	35.2	55.1	43.0	24.6	50.0	32.9
	×	×	×		59.0	54.3	56.6	60.1	64.5	62.2	58.3	65.4	61.6	57.3	66.6	61.6
	×	×	×	×	59.0	54.3	56.6	61.8	65.1	63.4	60.8	66.3	63.4	59.8	67.5	63.4
×					20.9	49.0	29.3	18.6	46.1	26.5	10.7	34.1	16.3	17.1	60.0	26.6
×				×	20.9	49.0	29.3	18.4	47.0	26.5	12.1	39.0	18.4	13.4	30.1	18.6
×			×		27.1	55.5	36.4	22.8	49.1	31.1	27.3	54.6	36.4	21.0	48.2	29.3
×			×	×	21.7	50.0	30.2	19.5	46.2	27.4	27.9	56.2	37.3	25.5	54.0	34.7
×		×			34.1	61.1	43.7	21.4	41.9	28.4	21.0	39.6	27.4	13.3	36.9	19.6
×		×		×	30.2	58.2	39.7	22.5	45.9	30.2	21.9	44.2	29.3	21.4	35.2	26.6
×		×	×		34.1	61.1	43.7	33.0	58.3	42.2	32.8	59.1	42.2	31.2	57.9	40.6
×		×	×	×	32.5	60.0	42.2	36.7	61.8	46.0	32.5	60.0	42.2	31.7	59.4	41.4
×	×				49.6	69.5	57.9	29.3	75.0	42.2	28.9	77.7	42.2	19.1	73.6	30.4
×	×			×	49.6	69.5	57.9	37.0	79.1	50.4	31.0	78.9	44.5	21.9	76.1	34.0
×	×		×		49.6	69.5	57.9	52.4	82.2	64.0	52.1	83.1	64.0	51.4	83.9	63.7
×	×		×	×	52.7	70.8	60.4	52.1	83.1	64.0	53.1	84.4	65.2	52.4	85.2	64.9
×	×	×			52.7	70.8	60.4	33.5	77.4	46.8	29.6	78.1	43.0	19.8	74.3	31.3
×	×	×		×	52.7	70.8	60.4	40.5	80.5	53.9	31.7	79.3	45.3	23.9	77.7	36.6
×	×	×	×		52.7	70.8	60.4	55.0	81.9	65.8	54.6	82.7	65.8	53.9	83.5	65.5
×	×	×	×	×	52.7	70.8	**60.4**	55.3	82.9	**66.3**	55.6	84.0	**66.9**	55.6	84.9	**67.2**

Table B.2: Partial-match accuracy results, broken down by activated features, use of grammar relaxation, and number of recognition hypotheses considered. For each configuration, we give the precision, recall, and F_1 value (all in percents).

Grammar Relaxation	Activated Features				Nbest 1			Nbest 3			Nbest 5			Nbest 10		
	Semantic	Syntactic	Acoustic	Contextual	Pr.	R.	F_1	Pr.	R.	F_1	Pr.	R.	F_1	Pr.	R.	F_1
					86.2	56.2	**68.0**	77.2	51.9	62.0	73.5	45.8	56.4	77.1	62.9	69.3
				×	85.5	56.0	67.7	81.7	55.3	66.0	81.3	54.2	65.1	74.7	52.7	61.8
			×		86.8	56.4	68.3	84.7	60.1	70.3	84.3	60.4	70.4	84.3	60.4	70.4
			×	×	86.2	56.2	68.1	84.0	59.5	69.7	85.4	60.4	70.7	83.9	60.0	70.0
		×			85.7	56.1	67.8	79.6	56.8	66.3	78.9	57.6	66.6	76.4	63.5	69.4
		×		×	86.8	56.4	68.3	81.8	57.4	67.5	78.9	55.9	65.5	76.3	51.7	61.6
		×	×		86.6	56.3	68.3	83.7	59.8	69.7	83.9	60.3	70.2	84.1	60.4	70.3
		×	×	×	87.4	56.6	68.7	83.5	59.4	69.4	85.0	60.3	70.5	83.8	59.9	69.9
	×				90.5	57.4	70.3	83.6	64.9	73.1	80.1	66.4	72.6	74.1	67.7	70.8
	×			×	90.5	57.4	70.3	85.5	65.4	74.1	83.3	67.2	74.4	80.9	69.6	74.8
	×		×		90.5	57.4	70.3	89.2	65.9	75.8	88.9	67.1	76.4	88.6	68.0	77.0
	×		×	×	90.5	57.4	70.3	89.6	66.0	76.0	89.5	67.2	76.8	89.3	68.2	77.3
	×	×			90.5	57.4	70.3	80.4	64.0	71.3	80.5	66.4	72.8	77.0	68.5	72.5
	×	×		×	90.5	57.4	70.3	82.8	64.7	72.6	80.1	66.4	72.6	78.1	68.8	73.2
	×	×	×		90.5	57.4	70.3	89.2	65.9	75.8	88.9	67.1	76.4	88.6	68.8	77.0
	×	×	×	×	90.5	57.4	70.3	89.6	66.0	76.0	89.5	67.2	76.8	89.3	68.2	77.3
×					75.7	73.3	74.5	71.0	78.1	74.4	71.4	81.9	76.3	67.0	83.9	74.5
×				×	73.7	72.8	73.2	71.5	76.8	74.1	71.7	78.7	75.1	69.4	66.7	68.0
×			×		75.3	73.2	74.2	75.7	72.7	74.1	74.6	73.1	73.8	74.3	73.0	73.7
×			×	×	72.7	72.5	72.6	74.1	73.3	73.7	74.6	74.1	74.4	74.4	74.1	74.2
×		×			80.9	74.6	77.6	76.7	71.8	74.2	76.2	72.1	74.1	73.7	77.4	75.5
×		×		×	80.2	74.4	77.2	78.3	74.5	76.3	78.7	76.2	77.4	72.8	65.9	69.2
×		×	×		80.8	74.6	77.6	81.0	74.0	77.3	80.3	74.5	77.3	79.0	74.2	76.5
×		×	×	×	80.4	74.5	77.3	80.7	74.9	77.7	80.3	75.5	77.8	79.9	75.4	77.6
×	×				86.5	75.8	80.8	81.3	86.5	83.8	80.7	88.4	84.4	73.4	89.9	80.8
×	×			×	86.5	75.8	80.8	82.8	86.7	84.7	80.0	88.3	84.0	77.6	90.4	83.5
×	×		×		86.5	75.8	80.8	86.4	85.9	86.2	86.2	86.7	86.4	86.0	87.7	86.9
×	×		×	×	86.5	75.8	80.8	86.2	86.4	86.3	86.3	87.2	86.8	86.2	88.3	87.2
×	×	×			88.1	76.2	81.7	82.0	86.6	84.3	79.3	88.2	83.5	77.9	90.4	83.7
×	×	×		×	88.1	76.2	81.7	83.9	86.8	85.3	81.7	88.5	85.0	80.1	90.6	85.0
×	×	×	×		88.1	76.2	81.7	87.8	84.7	86.2	87.5	85.4	86.4	87.4	86.4	86.9
×	×	×	×	×	88.1	76.2	**81.7**	87.6	85.2	**86.4**	87.6	86.0	**86.8**	87.7	87.0	**87.3**

Table B.3: Word Error Rate results, broken down by activated features, use of grammar relaxation, and number of recognition hypotheses considered. For each configuration, we give the word error rate, in percents.

Grammar Relaxation	Activated Features				Nbest 1	Nbest 3	Nbest 5	Nbest 10
	Semantic	Syntactic	Acoustic	Contextual				
					20.5	**26.9**	**29.7**	**25.9**
				×	20.5	23.6	24.6	28.0
			×		20.5	19.7	19.6	19.7
			×	×	20.5	18.7	18.2	18.3
		×			20.5	27.1	27.4	26.6
		×		×	20.5	24.9	25.3	28.4
		×	×		20.5	19.7	19.6	19.7
		×	×	×	20.5	18.7	18.4	18.3
	×				20.5	24.6	25.6	31.2
	×			×	20.5	21.4	23.2	26.1
	×		×		20.5	18.3	18.4	18.1
	×		×	×	20.5	17.3	17.4	17.4
	×	×			20.5	23.6	26.2	30.6
	×	×		×	20.5	20.3	23.1	27.0
	×	×	×		20.5	18.3	18.4	18.1
	×	×	×	×	20.5	17.6	17.2	17.4
×					19.6	23.6	25.9	23.9
×				×	19.3	20.4	23.3	26.7
×			×		19.7	18.6	18.4	19.3
×			×	×	19.4	18.0	17.6	17.7
×		×			19.4	24.6	26.9	27.9
×		×		×	19.4	22.2	23.9	28.1
×		×	×		19.4	18.8	18.7	18.8
×		×	×	×	19.4	17.8	17.3	17.4
×	×				20.2	22.4	25.5	29.4
×	×			×	20.2	21.0	22.9	26.1
×	×		×		20.2	17.8	17.8	17.8
×	×		×	×	19.4	17.4	17.1	17.1
×	×	×			19.4	21.5	24.3	28.7
×	×	×		×	19.4	19.8	21.9	25.9
×	×	×	×		19.4	16.8	16.7	16.7
×	×	×	×	×	**19.4**	**16.5**	**15.7**	**15.7**

136

B.2 Figures

We present below various figures which illustrates graphically the results we achieved for the parse selection task. The data used to generate the graphs is the same as the one shown in the tables B.1, B.2, and B.3.

B.2.1 Global results with all NBest hypotheses

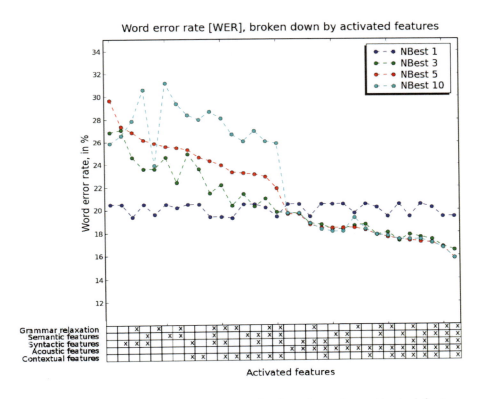

Figure B.1: Word error rate, broken down by activated features.

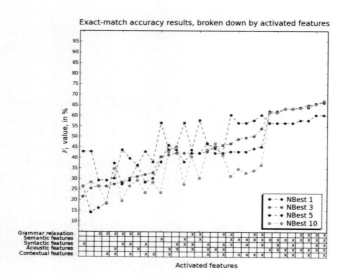

Figure B.2: F_1 values for exact-match, broken down by activated features.

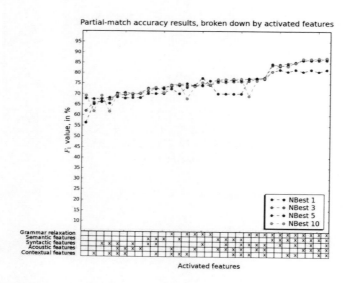

Figure B.3: F_1 values for exact-match, broken down by activated features.

B.2.2 Detailed results for exact-match

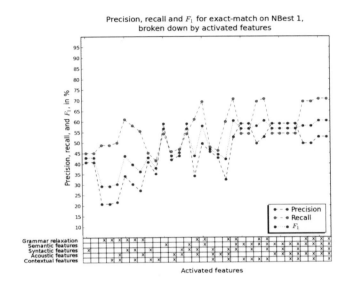

Figure B.4: Precision, Recall and F_1 for exact-match on NBest 1

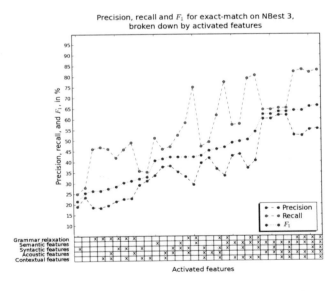

Figure B.5: Precision, Recall and F_1 for exact-match on NBest 3

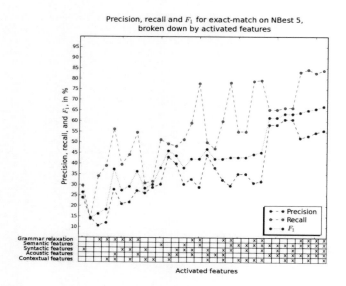

Figure B.6: Precision, Recall and F_1 for exact-match on NBest 5

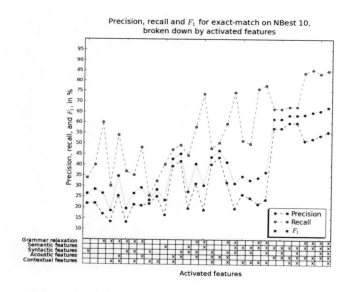

Figure B.7: Precision, Recall and F_1 for exact-match on NBest 10

B.2.3 Detailed results for partial-match

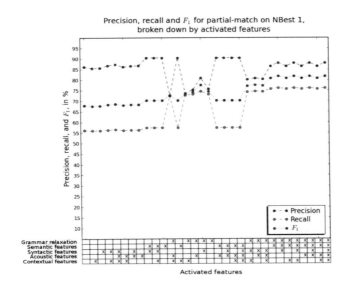

Figure B.8: Precision, Recall and F_1 for partial-match on NBest 1

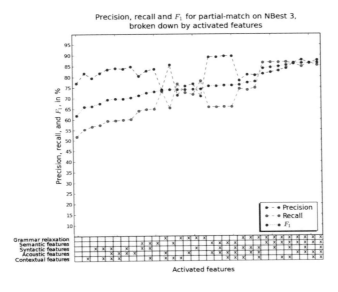

Figure B.9: Precision, Recall and F_1 for partial-match on NBest 3

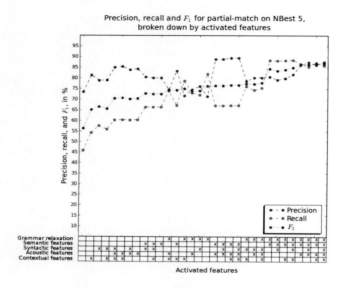

Figure B.10: Precision, Recall and F_1 for partial-match on NBest 5

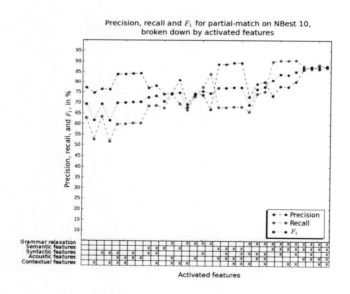

Figure B.11: Precision, Recall and F_1 for partial-match on NBest 10

C

Domain-specific grammar for corpus generation

We provide here some technical details about the domain-specific grammar used to automatically generate the training examples of our algorithm (cfr 6.3.1). The grammar serves as a resource to produce a set of training examples $\{x_i, z_i\}$ – where x_i is an utterance and z_i its associated semantics.

Each rule is weighted. The stipulation of the weights is realised by parsing the transcripts of the Wizard of Oz experiments at our disposal, and counting the relative use of each rule.

Once the grammar is specified and weighted, the generation of the training examples $\{x_i, z_i\}$ is done by simply traversing the grammar a large number of times and recording the results.

C.1 Definitions

The grammar is a familiar **context-free grammar**, where each rule is associated to a particular *semantic representation* as well as to a *weight*. It is formally defined as a tuple $G = \{V, \Sigma, M, R, S\}$, where:

context-free grammar

- V is an alphabet (finite set of symbols);

- $\Sigma \subseteq V$ is the set of terminal symbols. $V - \Sigma$ is therefore the set of non-terminal symbols.

- M is the space of possible semantic representations (i.e. logical forms). Each instance of M is a formula expressed in the HLDS formalism (cf. Chapter 4). It is defined as a tuple $\{Noms, root\}$, where:

    1. $Noms$ is a set of nominals. Each nominal includes an identifier, an ontological sort, a logical proposition, a set of features and a set of dependency relations.

143

2. *root* is a reference to the root nominal.

- $R \subseteq (V \times V^+ \times M \times \Re)$ is the set of context-free rules, associated with their semantic counterpart ($\in M$) and their weight ($\in \Re$).

- S is the start symbol.

plug-in nominals

A particular characteristic of the logical forms used here is the presence of "plug-in nominals". The content of these nominals is defined relative to the non-terminals specified in the right-hand side of the rule. Consider for instance the following rule:

$$\text{COMMAND-DIRECT} \Rightarrow \text{move OBJ}_{\boxed{2}} \tag{C.1}$$

The semantics of rule C.1 is defined as such:

$$@_{c:\text{action-motion}}(\mathbf{move} \wedge \langle \text{PATIENT}\rangle(\boxed{2})) \tag{C.2}$$

The symbol $\boxed{2}$ represents a plug-in nominal. It indicates that the semantics associated to the non-terminal "OBJ" needs to be "plugged-in" in the representation to complete the logical form.

C.2 Grammar specification

We present below the specification of our grammar. Due to space constraints, only one third of the total number of rules are listed here.

On the left, we indicate the syntactic derivation (for ease of presentation, the elements in the right-hand side of the rule are listed vertically). The non-terminals are shown in uppercase, the terminals in lowercase.

On the right, we indicate the associated semantic representation.

Syntactic derivation	Associated HLDS semantics
S $\Rightarrow$ CONTENT$_{\boxed{1}}$	$@(\boxed{1})$
S $\Rightarrow$ DISFL$_{\boxed{1}}$ CONTENT$_{\boxed{2}}$	$@(@(\boxed{2}))$
S $\Rightarrow$ TEMPORAL-LC$_{\boxed{1}}$ CONTENT$_{\boxed{2}}$	$@(\boxed{2} \wedge$ $\langle \text{MODIFIER}\rangle(\boxed{1}))$
S $\Rightarrow$ DISC-PARTICLE$_{\boxed{1}}$ CONTENT$_{\boxed{2}}$	$@_{s1:\text{d-units}}(\mathbf{list} \wedge$ $\langle \text{FIRST}\rangle(\boxed{1}) \wedge$ $\langle \text{NEXT}\rangle(\boxed{2}))$

S ⇒ CONTENT[1] 　　　DISC–PARTICLE[2]	$@_{s1:\text{d-units}}(\textbf{list} \land$ 　$\langle\text{FIRST}\rangle(\boxed{1}) \land$ 　$\langle\text{NEXT}\rangle(\boxed{2}))$
S ⇒ DISC–PARTICLE[1] 　　　TEMPORAL–LC[2] 　　　CONTENT[3]	$@_{s1:\text{d-units}}(\textbf{list} \land$ 　$\langle\text{FIRST}\rangle(\boxed{1}) \land$ 　$\langle\text{NEXT}\rangle(\boxed{3} \land$ 　　$\langle\text{MODIFIER}\rangle(\boxed{2})))$
S ⇒ DISC–PARTICLE[1] 　　　DISC–PARTICLE[2] 　　　CONTENT[3]	$@_{s2:\text{d-units}}(\textbf{list} \land$ 　$\langle\text{FIRST}\rangle(\boxed{1}) \land$ 　$\langle\text{NEXT}\rangle(s3:\text{d-units} \land \textbf{list} \land$ 　　$\langle\text{FIRST}\rangle(\boxed{2}) \land$ 　　$\langle\text{NEXT}\rangle(\boxed{3})))$
CONTENT ⇒ GREETING[1]	$@(\boxed{1})$
CONTENT ⇒ COMMAND[1]	$@(\boxed{1})$
CONTENT ⇒ ASSERTION[1]	$@(\boxed{1})$
CONTENT ⇒ QUESTION[1]	$@(\boxed{1})$
CONTENT ⇒ EVALUATION[1]	$@(\boxed{1})$
CONTENT ⇒ OBJ[1]	$@(\boxed{1})$
CONTENT ⇒ QUALIFIER[1]	$@(\boxed{1})$
CONTENT ⇒ LOCATION–MOD[1]	$@(\boxed{1})$
CONTENT ⇒ MISC[1]	$@(\boxed{1})$
DISC–PARTICLE ⇒ x with $x \in \{\textbf{and, now, so, well}\}$	$@_{m1:\text{marker}}(y)$ with $y \in \{\textbf{and, now, so, well}\}$
DISC–PARTICLE ⇒ CUEWORD–MARKER[1]	$@(\boxed{1})$
DISC–PARTICLE ⇒ PERSON–LC[1]	$@(\boxed{1})$
DISFL ⇒ x with $x \in \{\textbf{uh, um, mm, err, ah}\}$	$@()$
MISC ⇒ i 　　　mean	$@_{misc1:\text{cognition}}(\textbf{mean} \land$ 　$\langle\text{MOOD}\rangle ind \land$ 　$\langle\text{TENSE}\rangle pres \land$ 　$\langle\text{ACTOR}\rangle(i1:\text{person} \land \textbf{I} \land$ 　　$\langle\text{NUM}\rangle sg) \land$ 　$\langle\text{EVENT}\rangle x1:\text{event} \land$ 　$\langle\text{SUBJECT}\rangle i1:\text{person})$

MISC ⇒ you know	$@_{\text{misc2:cognition}}(\textbf{know} \wedge$ $\langle\text{MOOD}\rangle ind \wedge$ $\langle\text{TENSE}\rangle pres \wedge$ $\langle\text{ACTOR}\rangle(\text{y1:person} \wedge \textbf{you} \wedge$ $\langle\text{NUM}\rangle sg) \wedge$ $\langle\text{SUBJECT}\rangle\text{y1:person})$
MISC ⇒ i see	$@_{\text{misc3:perception}}(\textbf{see} \wedge$ $\langle\text{MOOD}\rangle ind \wedge$ $\langle\text{TENSE}\rangle pres \wedge$ $\langle\text{ACTOR}\rangle(\text{i1:person} \wedge \textbf{I} \wedge$ $\langle\text{NUM}\rangle sg) \wedge$ $\langle\text{SUBJECT}\rangle\text{i1:person})$
GREETING ⇒ hi	$@_{\text{g1:greeting}}(\textbf{hi})$
GREETING ⇒ hello	$@_{\text{g2:greeting}}(\textbf{hi})$
TEMPORAL–LC ⇒ now	$@_{\text{t1:m-time-point}}(\textbf{now})$
TEMPORAL–LC ⇒ x with $x \in \{\textbf{first}, \textbf{after}, \textbf{then}, \textbf{next}\}$	$@_{\text{t2:m-time-sequence}}(y)$ with $y \in \{\textbf{first}, \textbf{after}, \textbf{then}, \textbf{next}\}$
TEMPORAL–LC ⇒ again	$@_{\text{t2:m-time-frequency}}(\textbf{again})$
CONNECTIVE–BINARY ⇒ x with $x \in \{\textbf{then}, \textbf{and}, \textbf{or}, \textbf{but}\}$	$@(y)$ with $y \in \{\textbf{then}, \textbf{and}, \textbf{or}, \textbf{but}\}$
COMMAND ⇒ COMMAND–DIRECT$_{\boxed{1}}$	$@(\boxed{1} \wedge$ $\langle\text{MOOD}\rangle imp \wedge$ $\langle\text{SUBJECT}\rangle(\text{a1:entity} \wedge \textbf{addressee}) \wedge$ $\langle\text{ACTOR}\rangle\text{a1:entity})$
COMMAND ⇒ ADV–LC$_{\boxed{1}}$ COMMAND–DIRECT$_{\boxed{2}}$	$@(\boxed{2} \wedge$ $\langle\text{MOOD}\rangle imp \wedge$ $\langle\text{SUBJECT}\rangle(\text{a1:entity} \wedge \textbf{addressee}) \wedge$ $\langle\text{ACTOR}\rangle\text{a1:entity} \wedge$ $\langle\text{MODIFIER}\rangle(\boxed{1}))$
COMMAND ⇒ COMMAND–DIRECT$_{\boxed{1}}$ CONNECTIVE–BINARY$_{\boxed{2}}$ COMMAND–DIRECT$_{\boxed{3}}$	$@_{\text{com2:event}}($ $\langle\text{MOOD}\rangle imp \wedge$ $\langle\text{SUBJECT}\rangle(\text{a1:entity} \wedge \textbf{addressee}) \wedge$ $\boxed{2} \wedge$ $\langle\text{FIRST}\rangle(\boxed{1} \wedge$ $\langle\text{ACTOR}\rangle\text{a1:entity}) \wedge$ $\langle\text{NEXT}\rangle(\boxed{3}))$
COMMAND ⇒ COMMAND–INDIRECT$_{\boxed{1}}$	$@(\boxed{1})$
COMMAND–DIRECT ⇒ ACTION–TRANS–LC$_{\boxed{1}}$ OBJ$_{\boxed{2}}$	$@(\boxed{1} \wedge$ $\langle\text{PATIENT}\rangle(\boxed{2}))$

COMMAND–DIRECT $\Rightarrow$ pick
         OBJ$_{\boxed{2}}$
         up
	@$_{c1:\text{action-non-motion}}$(**pick** $\wedge$
	 $\langle\text{PATIENT}\rangle(\boxed{2})\ \wedge$
	 $\langle\text{PARTICLE}\rangle(u1\ \wedge \mathbf{up}))$

COMMAND–DIRECT $\Rightarrow$ listen	@$_{c2:\text{perception}}$(**listen**)
COMMAND–DIRECT $\Rightarrow$ look	@$_{c3:\text{perception}}$(**look**)
COMMAND–DIRECT $\Rightarrow$ look	@$_{c3:\text{action-non-motion}}$(**search**)

COMMAND–DIRECT $\Rightarrow$ look
         at
         OBJ$_{\boxed{3}}$
	@$_{c20:\text{perception}}$(**look** $\wedge$
	 $\langle\text{MODIFIER}\rangle(a1\text{:m-location}\ \wedge \mathbf{at}\ \wedge$
	 $\langle\text{ANCHOR}\rangle(\boxed{3})))$

COMMAND–DIRECT $\Rightarrow$ move OBJ$_{\boxed{2}}$	@$_{c4:\text{action-motion}}$(**move** $\wedge$ $\langle\text{PATIENT}\rangle(\boxed{2}))$

COMMAND–DIRECT $\Rightarrow$ move
         OBJ$_{\boxed{2}}$
         LOCATION-RESULT$_{\boxed{3}}$
	@$_{c5:\text{action-motion}}$(**move** $\wedge$
	 $\langle\text{PATIENT}\rangle(\boxed{2})\ \wedge$
	 $\langle\text{RESULT}\rangle(\boxed{3}))$

COMMAND–DIRECT $\Rightarrow$ put
         OBJ$_{\boxed{2}}$
         LOCATION-RESULT$_{\boxed{3}}$
	@$_{c6:\text{action-non-motion}}$(**put** $\wedge$
	 $\langle\text{PATIENT}\rangle(\boxed{2})\ \wedge$
	 $\langle\text{RESULT}\rangle(\boxed{3}))$

COMMAND–DIRECT $\Rightarrow$ give
         OBJ$_{\boxed{2}}$
         to
         PERSON-LC$_{\boxed{4}}$
	@$_{a5:\text{action-non-motion}}$(**give** $\wedge$
	 $\langle\text{PATIENT}\rangle(\boxed{2})\ \wedge$
	 $\langle\text{RECIPIENT}\rangle(\boxed{4}))$

COMMAND–DIRECT $\Rightarrow$ stop	@$_{a10:\text{modal}}$(**stop**)
COMMAND–DIRECT $\Rightarrow$ stop it	@$_{a10:\text{modal}}$(**stop** $\wedge$ $\langle\text{EVENT}\rangle(c25\text{:event}\ \wedge \mathbf{context}))$
ACTION–TRANS–LC $\Rightarrow$ x with $x \in \{\mathbf{take, reach, pick, get, open,}$ $\mathbf{close, play, rotate, remove, see}\}$	@$_{c1:\text{action-non-motion}}(y)$ with $\in \{\mathbf{take, reach, pick, get, open,}$ $\mathbf{close, play, rotate, remove, see}\}$
ACTION–TRANS–LC $\Rightarrow$ give me	@$_{c6:\text{action-non-motion}}$(**give** $\wedge$ $\langle\text{RECIPIENT}\rangle(i1\text{:person}\ \wedge \mathbf{I} \wedge$ $\langle\text{NUM}\rangle sg))$
ACTION–TRANS–LC $\Rightarrow$ get me	@$_{c8:\text{action-non-motion}}$(**get** $\wedge$ $\langle\text{RECIPIENT}\rangle(i1\text{:person}\ \wedge \mathbf{I} \wedge$ $\langle\text{NUM}\rangle sg))$
MODAL $\Rightarrow$ x with $x \in \{\mathbf{must, can, could, should, would}\}$	@$(\langle\text{TENSE}\rangle pres\ \wedge$ $\langle\text{MODIFIER}\rangle(\text{mod1:modal}\ \wedge y))$ with $y \in \{\mathbf{must, can, could, should,}$ $\mathbf{would}\}$

COMMAND−INDIRECT ⇒	MODAL$_{\boxed{1}}$ you COMMAND−DIRECT$_{\boxed{3}}$	@($\boxed{3}$ ∧ $\boxed{1}$ ∧ ⟨MOOD⟩int ∧ ⟨SUBJECT⟩(y1:person ∧ **you** ∧ ⟨NUM⟩sg) ∧ ⟨ACTOR⟩y1:person)
COMMAND−INDIRECT ⇒	you MODAL$_{\boxed{2}}$ COMMAND−DIRECT$_{\boxed{3}}$	@($\boxed{3}$ ∧ $\boxed{2}$ ∧ ⟨MOOD⟩ind ∧ ⟨SUBJECT⟩(y1:person ∧ **you** ∧ ⟨NUM⟩sg) ∧ ⟨ACTOR⟩y1:person)
COMMAND−INDIRECT ⇒	i want you to COMMAND−DIRECT$_{\boxed{5}}$	@$_{ci2:cognition}$(**want** ∧ ⟨MOOD⟩ind ∧ ⟨TENSE⟩$pres$ ∧ ⟨ACTOR⟩(i1:person ∧ **I** ∧ ⟨NUM⟩sg) ∧ ⟨EVENT⟩($\boxed{5}$ ∧ ⟨ACTOR⟩y1:person) ∧ ⟨SUBJECT⟩i1:person ∧ ⟨PATIENT⟩(y1:person ∧ **you** ∧ ⟨NUM⟩sg))
COMMAND−INDIRECT ⇒	MODAL$_{\boxed{1}}$ you ADV−LC$_{\boxed{3}}$ COMMAND−DIRECT$_{\boxed{4}}$	@($\boxed{4}$ ∧ $\boxed{1}$ ∧ ⟨MOOD⟩int ∧ ⟨SUBJECT⟩(y1:person ∧ **you** ∧ ⟨NUM⟩sg) ∧ ⟨ACTOR⟩y1:person ∧ ⟨MODIFIER⟩($\boxed{3}$))
COMMAND−INDIRECT ⇒	i want OBJ$_{\boxed{3}}$	@$_{ci3:cognition}$(**want** ∧ ⟨MOOD⟩ind ∧ ⟨TENSE⟩$pres$ ∧ ⟨ACTOR⟩(i1:person ∧ **I** ∧ ⟨NUM⟩sg) ∧ ⟨PATIENT⟩($\boxed{3}$) ∧ ⟨SUBJECT⟩i1:person)
COMMAND−INDIRECT ⇒	do not COMMAND−DIRECT$_{\boxed{3}}$	@($\boxed{3}$ ∧ ⟨MOOD⟩imp ∧ ⟨SUBJECT⟩(a1:entity ∧ **addressee**) ∧ ⟨POLARITY⟩neg)
PRONOUNS ⇒ with $x \in \{$i, you$\}$	x	@$_{i1:person}$(y ∧ ⟨NUM⟩sg) with $y \in \{$**i**, **you**$\}$
PRONOUNS ⇒	we	@$_{i1:person}$(**I** ∧ ⟨NUM⟩pl)
ADV−LC ⇒	just	@$_{a1:m-time}$(**just**)
ADV−LC ⇒	never	@$_{n1:m-frequency}$(**never**)
ADV−LC ⇒	also	@$_{a1:m-comment}$(**also**)
ADV−LC ⇒	please	@$_{a1:m-comment}$(**please**)

ADV-LC ⇒ already	$@_{a1:\text{m-time}}(\textbf{already})$

ASSERTION ⇒	PRONOUNS$_{\boxed{1}}$ see OBJ$_{\boxed{3}}$	$@_{as1:\text{perception}}(\textbf{see} \wedge$ $\langle \text{MOOD} \rangle ind \wedge$ $\langle \text{TENSE} \rangle pres \wedge$ $\langle \text{ACTOR} \rangle (\boxed{1}) \wedge$ $\langle \text{PATIENT} \rangle (\boxed{3}) \wedge$ $\langle \text{SUBJECT} \rangle (\boxed{1}))$
ASSERTION ⇒	LOCATION-MOD$_{\boxed{1}}$ is OBJ-SG$_{\boxed{3}}$	$@_{as3:\text{presentational}}(\textbf{be} \wedge$ $\langle \text{MOOD} \rangle ind \wedge$ $\langle \text{TENSE} \rangle pres \wedge$ $\langle \text{MODIFIER} \rangle (\boxed{1}) \wedge$ $\langle \text{PRESENTED} \rangle (\boxed{3}))$
ASSERTION ⇒	LOCATION-MOD$_{\boxed{1}}$ are OBJ-PL$_{\boxed{3}}$	$@_{as5:\text{presentational}}(\textbf{be} \wedge$ $\langle \text{MOOD} \rangle ind \wedge$ $\langle \text{TENSE} \rangle pres \wedge$ $\langle \text{MODIFIER} \rangle (\boxed{1}) \wedge$ $\langle \text{PRESENTED} \rangle (\boxed{3}))$
ASSERTION ⇒	OBJ-SG$_{\boxed{1}}$ is LOCATION-MOD$_{\boxed{3}}$	$@_{as7:\text{ascription}}(\textbf{be} \wedge$ $\langle \text{MOOD} \rangle ind \wedge$ $\langle \text{TENSE} \rangle pres \wedge$ $\langle \text{COP-RESTR} \rangle (\boxed{1}) \wedge$ $\langle \text{COP-SCOPE} \rangle (\boxed{3}) \wedge$ $\langle \text{SUBJECT} \rangle (\boxed{1}))$
ASSERTION ⇒	OBJ-SG$_{\boxed{1}}$ is ADV-LC$_{\boxed{3}}$ LOCATION-MOD$_{\boxed{4}}$	$@_{as8:\text{ascription}}(\textbf{be} \wedge$ $\langle \text{MOOD} \rangle ind \wedge$ $\langle \text{TENSE} \rangle pres \wedge$ $\langle \text{COP-RESTR} \rangle (\boxed{1}) \wedge$ $\langle \text{MODIFIER} \rangle (\boxed{3}) \wedge$ $\langle \text{COP-SCOPE} \rangle (\boxed{4}) \wedge$ $\langle \text{SUBJECT} \rangle (\boxed{1}))$
ASSERTION ⇒	PRONOUNS$_{\boxed{1}}$ have OBJ$_{\boxed{3}}$	$@_{as10:\text{ascription}}(\textbf{have} \wedge$ $\langle \text{MOOD} \rangle ind \wedge$ $\langle \text{TENSE} \rangle pres \wedge$ $\langle \text{ACTOR} \rangle (\boxed{1}) \wedge$ $\langle \text{PATIENT} \rangle (\boxed{3}) \wedge$ $\langle \text{SUBJECT} \rangle (\boxed{1}))$
ASSERTION ⇒	OBJ-SG$_{\boxed{1}}$ is QUALIFIER$_{\boxed{3}}$	$@_{as11:\text{ascription}}(\textbf{be} \wedge$ $\langle \text{MOOD} \rangle ind \wedge$ $\langle \text{TENSE} \rangle pres \wedge$ $\langle \text{COP-RESTR} \rangle (\boxed{1}) \wedge$ $\langle \text{COP-SCOPE} \rangle (\boxed{3}) \wedge$ $\langle \text{SUBJECT} \rangle (\boxed{1}))$
ASSERTION ⇒	OBJ-SG$_{\boxed{1}}$ is not QUALIFIER$_{\boxed{4}}$	$@_{as12:\text{ascription}}(\textbf{be} \wedge$ $\langle \text{MOOD} \rangle ind \wedge$ $\langle \text{TENSE} \rangle pres \wedge$ $\langle \text{COP-RESTR} \rangle (\boxed{1}) \wedge$ $\langle \text{POLARITY} \rangle (neg) \wedge$ $\langle \text{COP-SCOPE} \rangle (\boxed{4}) \wedge$ $\langle \text{SUBJECT} \rangle (\boxed{1}))$

ASSERTION ⇒ OBJ-SG[1] is OBJ-SG[3]	$@_{as18:ascription}(\mathbf{be} \wedge$ $\langle \text{MOOD} \rangle ind \wedge$ $\langle \text{TENSE} \rangle pres \wedge$ $\langle \text{COP-RESTR} \rangle ([1]) \wedge$ $\langle \text{COP-SCOPE} \rangle ([3]) \wedge$ $\langle \text{SUBJECT} \rangle ([1]))$
ASSERTION ⇒ OBJ-SG[1] is not OBJ-SG[4]	$@_{as19:ascription}(\mathbf{be} \wedge$ $\langle \text{MOOD} \rangle ind \wedge$ $\langle \text{TENSE} \rangle pres \wedge$ $\langle \text{COP-RESTR} \rangle ([1]) \wedge$ $\langle \text{POLARITY} \rangle neg \wedge$ $\langle \text{COP-SCOPE} \rangle ([4]) \wedge$ $\langle \text{SUBJECT} \rangle ([1]))$
ASSERTION ⇒ DEM-PL[1] are OBJ-PL[3]	$@_{as16:ascription}(\mathbf{be} \wedge$ $\langle \text{MOOD} \rangle ind \wedge$ $\langle \text{TENSE} \rangle pres \wedge$ $\langle \text{COP-RESTR} \rangle ([1]) \wedge$ $\langle \text{COP-SCOPE} \rangle ([3]) \wedge$ $\langle \text{SUBJECT} \rangle ([1]))$
ASSERTION ⇒ OBJ-PL[1] are QUALIFIER[3]	$@_{as11:ascription}(\mathbf{be} \wedge$ $\langle \text{MOOD} \rangle ind \wedge$ $\langle \text{TENSE} \rangle pres \wedge$ $\langle \text{COP-RESTR} \rangle ([1]) \wedge$ $\langle \text{COP-SCOPE} \rangle ([3]) \wedge$ $\langle \text{SUBJECT} \rangle ([1]))$
OBJ ⇒ OBJ-SG[1]	$@([1])$
OBJ ⇒ OBJ-PL[1]	$@([1])$
OBJ-SG ⇒ DEM-SG-PRONOUN[1]	$@([1])$
OBJ-SG ⇒ DET-SG[1] OBJ-SG-LC[2]	$@([2] \wedge [1])$
OBJ-SG ⇒ DET-SG[1] QUALIFIER[2] OBJ-SG-LC[3]	$@([3] \wedge [1] \wedge$ $\langle \text{MODIFIER} \rangle ([2]))$
OBJ-SG ⇒ DET-SG[1] OBJ-SG-LC[2] LOCATION-MOD[3]	$@([2] \wedge [1] \wedge$ $\langle \text{MODIFIER} \rangle ([3]))$
OBJ-SG ⇒ DET-SG[1] ADJUNCT-LC[2] OBJ-SG-LC[3] LOCATION-MOD[4]	$@([3] \wedge [1] \wedge$ $\langle \text{MODIFIER} \rangle ([2]) \wedge$ $\langle \text{MODIFIER} \rangle ([4]))$
OBJ-SG ⇒ something	$@_{o1:thing}(\mathbf{context} \wedge$ $\langle \text{DELIMITATION} \rangle existential \wedge$ $\langle \text{NUM} \rangle sg \wedge$ $\langle \text{QUANTIFICATION} \rangle specific)$
OBJ-SG ⇒ it	$@_{o4:thing}(\mathbf{it} \wedge$ $\langle \text{NUM} \rangle sg)$

OBJ–SG $\Rightarrow$ one	$@_{o6:\text{entity}}(\textbf{context} \land$ $\quad \langle\text{DELIMITATION}\rangle existential \land$ $\quad \langle\text{NUM}\rangle sg \land$ $\quad \langle\text{QUANTIFICATION}\rangle specific \land$ $\quad \langle\text{MODIFIER}\rangle(\text{n1:number–cardinal} \land 1))$
OBJ–SG $\Rightarrow$ DET–SG$_{\boxed{1}}$ OBJ–SG–LC$_{\boxed{2}}$ of PERSON–LC$_{\boxed{4}}$	$@(\boxed{2} \land \boxed{1} \land$ $\quad \langle\text{OWNER}\rangle(\boxed{4}))$
OBJ–PL $\Rightarrow$ DEM–PL–PRONOUN$_{\boxed{1}}$	$@(\boxed{1})$
OBJ–PL $\Rightarrow$ DET–PL$_{\boxed{1}}$ OBJ–PL–LC$_{\boxed{2}}$	$@(\boxed{2} \land \boxed{1})$
OBJ–PL $\Rightarrow$ DET–PL$_{\boxed{1}}$ ADJUNCT–LC$_{\boxed{2}}$ OBJ–PL–LC$_{\boxed{3}}$	$@(\boxed{3} \land \boxed{1} \land$ $\quad \langle\text{MODIFIER}\rangle(\boxed{2}))$
OBJ–PL $\Rightarrow$ DET–PL$_{\boxed{1}}$ OBJ–PL–LC$_{\boxed{2}}$ LOCATION–MOD$_{\boxed{3}}$	$@(\boxed{2} \land \boxed{1} \land$ $\quad \langle\text{MODIFIER}\rangle(\boxed{3}))$
OBJ–PL $\Rightarrow$ OBJ$_{\boxed{1}}$ and OBJ$_{\boxed{3}}$	$@_{e1:\text{entity}}(\textbf{and} \land$ $\quad \langle\text{NUM}\rangle pl \land$ $\quad \langle\text{FIRST}\rangle(\boxed{1}) \land$ $\quad \langle\text{NEXT}\rangle(\boxed{3}))$
DET–SG $\Rightarrow$ DET–SG–LC$_{\boxed{1}}$	$@(\boxed{1})$
DET–SG $\Rightarrow$ DEM–SG–LC$_{\boxed{1}}$	$@(\boxed{1})$
DET–PL $\Rightarrow$ DET–PL–LC$_{\boxed{1}}$	$@(\boxed{1})$
DET–PL $\Rightarrow$ DEM–PL–LC$_{\boxed{1}}$	$@(\boxed{1})$
QUESTION $\Rightarrow$ where is OBJ–SG$_{\boxed{3}}$	$@_{q1:\text{ascription}}(\textbf{be} \land$ $\quad \langle\text{MOOD}\rangle int \land$ $\quad \langle\text{TENSE}\rangle pres \land$ $\quad \langle\text{COP–RESTR}\rangle(\boxed{3}) \land$ $\quad \langle\text{COP–SCOPE}\rangle(\text{w1:m–location} \land$ $\quad\quad \textbf{where}) \land$ $\quad \langle\text{SUBJECT}\rangle(\boxed{3}) \land$ $\quad \langle\text{WH–RESTR}\rangle\text{w1:m–location})$
QUESTION $\Rightarrow$ where are OBJ–PL$_{\boxed{3}}$	$@_{q2:\text{ascription}}(\textbf{be} \land$ $\quad \langle\text{MOOD}\rangle int \land$ $\quad \langle\text{TENSE}\rangle pres \land$ $\quad \langle\text{COP–RESTR}\rangle(\boxed{3}) \land$ $\quad \langle\text{COP–SCOPE}\rangle(\text{w1:m–location} \land$ $\quad\quad \textbf{where}) \land$ $\quad \langle\text{SUBJECT}\rangle(\boxed{3}) \land$ $\quad \langle\text{WH–RESTR}\rangle\text{w1:m–location})$

QUESTION ⇒	what
	do
	you
	see
		@$_{q5:perception}$(**see** ∧
		  ⟨MOOD⟩int ∧
		  ⟨TENSE⟩$pres$ ∧
		  ⟨ACTOR⟩(y1:person ∧ **you** ∧
		    ⟨NUM⟩sg) ∧
		  ⟨PATIENT⟩(w1:entity ∧ **what**) ∧
		  ⟨SUBJECT⟩y1:person ∧
		  ⟨WH-RESTR⟩w1:entity)

QUESTION ⇒	do
	you
	see
	OBJ$_{[4]}$
		@$_{q7:perception}$(**see** ∧
		  ⟨MOOD⟩int ∧
		  ⟨TENSE⟩$pres$ ∧
		  ⟨ACTOR⟩(y1:person ∧ **you** ∧
		    ⟨NUM⟩sg) ∧
		  ⟨PATIENT⟩([4]) ∧
		  ⟨SUBJECT⟩y1:person)

QUESTION ⇒	do
	you
	see
	OBJ$_{[4]}$
	LOCATION-MOD$_{[5]}$
		@$_{q7:perception}$(**see** ∧
		  ⟨MOOD⟩int ∧
		  ⟨TENSE⟩$pres$ ∧
		  ⟨ACTOR⟩(y1:person ∧ **you** ∧
		    ⟨NUM⟩sg) ∧
		  ⟨PATIENT⟩([4]) ∧
		  ⟨SUBJECT⟩y1:person ∧
		  ⟨MODIFIER⟩([5]))

QUESTION ⇒	what
	colour
	is
	OBJ-SG$_{[4]}$
		@$_{q8:ascription}$(**be** ∧
		  ⟨MOOD⟩int ∧
		  ⟨TENSE⟩$pres$ ∧
		  ⟨COP-RESTR⟩([4]) ∧
		  ⟨COP-SCOPE⟩(c1:quality ∧ **color**) ∧
		  ⟨SUBJECT⟩([4]) ∧
		  ⟨WH-RESTR⟩(w1:specifier ∧
		    what ∧
		    ⟨SCOPE⟩c1:quality))

QUESTION ⇒	what
	size
	is
	OBJ-SG$_{[4]}$
		@$_{q10:ascription}$(**be** ∧
		  ⟨MOOD⟩int ∧
		  ⟨TENSE⟩$pres$ ∧
		  ⟨COP-RESTR⟩([4]) ∧
		  ⟨COP-SCOPE⟩(c1:quality ∧ **size**) ∧
		  ⟨SUBJECT⟩([4]) ∧
		  ⟨WH-RESTR⟩(w1:specifier ∧
		    what ∧
		    ⟨SCOPE⟩c1:quality))

QUESTION ⇒	how
	ADJUNCT-LC$_{[2]}$
	is
	OBJ-SG$_{[4]}$
		@$_{q12:ascription}$(**be** ∧
		  ⟨MOOD⟩int ∧
		  ⟨TENSE⟩$pres$ ∧
		  ⟨COP-RESTR⟩([4]) ∧
		  ⟨COP-SCOPE⟩([2]) ∧
		  ⟨SUBJECT⟩([2]) ∧
		  ⟨WH-RESTR⟩(h1:quality ∧ **how** ∧
		    ⟨SCOPE⟩([2])))

QUESTION $\Rightarrow$	how is OBJ-SG$_{\boxed{3}}$	$@_{q13:ascription}($ **be** $\wedge$ $\langle$MOOD$\rangle int \wedge$ $\langle$TENSE$\rangle pres \wedge$ $\langle$COP-RESTR$\rangle(\boxed{3}) \wedge$ $\langle$COP-SCOPE$\rangle$(h1:quality $\wedge$ **how**) $\wedge$ $\langle$SUBJECT$\rangle(\boxed{3}) \wedge$ $\langle$WH-RESTR$\rangle$h1:quality)
QUESTION $\Rightarrow$	what is LOCATION-MOD$_{\boxed{3}}$	$@_{q15:ascription}($ **be** $\wedge$ $\langle$MOOD$\rangle int \wedge$ $\langle$TENSE$\rangle pres \wedge$ $\langle$COP-RESTR$\rangle$(w1:entity $\wedge$ **what**) $\wedge$ $\langle$COP-SCOPE$\rangle(\boxed{3}) \wedge$ $\langle$SUBJECT$\rangle$w1:entity $\wedge$ $\langle$WH-RESTR$\rangle$w1:entity)
QUESTION $\Rightarrow$	what is OBJ-SG$_{\boxed{3}}$	$@_{q24:ascription}($ **be** $\wedge$ $\langle$MOOD$\rangle int \wedge$ $\langle$TENSE$\rangle pres \wedge$ $\langle$COP-RESTR$\rangle(\boxed{3}) \wedge$ $\langle$COP-SCOPE$\rangle$(w1:entity $\wedge$ **what**) $\wedge$ $\langle$SUBJECT$\rangle(\boxed{3}) \wedge$ $\langle$WH-RESTR$\rangle$w1:entity)
QUESTION $\Rightarrow$	is OBJ-SG$_{\boxed{2}}$ QUALIFIER$_{\boxed{3}}$	$@_{q16:ascription}($ **be** $\wedge$ $\langle$MOOD$\rangle int \wedge$ $\langle$TENSE$\rangle pres \wedge$ $\langle$COP-RESTR$\rangle(\boxed{2}) \wedge$ $\langle$COP-SCOPE$\rangle(\boxed{3}) \wedge$ $\langle$SUBJECT$\rangle(\boxed{2})$))
QUESTION $\Rightarrow$	are OBJ-PL$_{\boxed{2}}$ QUALIFIER$_{\boxed{3}}$	$@_{q17:ascription}($ **be** $\wedge$ $\langle$MOOD$\rangle int \wedge$ $\langle$TENSE$\rangle pres \wedge$ $\langle$COP-RESTR$\rangle(\boxed{2}) \wedge$ $\langle$COP-SCOPE$\rangle(\boxed{3}) \wedge$ $\langle$SUBJECT$\rangle(\boxed{2})$))
QUESTION $\Rightarrow$	is OBJ-SG$_{\boxed{2}}$ LOCATION-MOD$_{\boxed{3}}$	$@_{q19:ascription}($ **be** $\wedge$ $\langle$MOOD$\rangle int \wedge$ $\langle$TENSE$\rangle pres \wedge$ $\langle$COP-RESTR$\rangle(\boxed{2}) \wedge$ $\langle$COP-SCOPE$\rangle(\boxed{3}) \wedge$ $\langle$SUBJECT$\rangle(\boxed{2})$))
QUESTION $\Rightarrow$	is there OBJ-SG$_{\boxed{3}}$ LOCATION-MOD$_{\boxed{4}}$	$@_{q21:presentational}($ **be** $\wedge$ $\langle$MOOD$\rangle int \wedge$ $\langle$TENSE$\rangle pres \wedge$ $\langle$MODIFIER$\rangle(\boxed{4}) \wedge$ $\langle$PRESENTED$\rangle(\boxed{3}) \wedge$ $\langle$SUBJECT$\rangle$(t1:dummy $\wedge$ **there**))

QUESTION ⇒ which
OBJ–SG–LC$_{\boxed{2}}$
is
QUALIFIER$_{\boxed{4}}$
	@$_{q23:ascription}$(be ∧
	  ⟨MOOD⟩int ∧
	  ⟨TENSE⟩$pres$ ∧
	  ⟨COP-RESTR⟩($\boxed{2}$ ∧
	    ⟨DELIMITATION⟩$unique$ ∧
	    ⟨QUANTIFICATION⟩$specific$) ∧
	  ⟨COP-SCOPE⟩($\boxed{4}$) ∧
	  ⟨SUBJECT⟩($\boxed{2}$) ∧
	  ⟨WH-RESTR⟩(w1:specifier ∧
	    which ∧
	    ⟨SCOPE⟩($\boxed{2}$)))

QUESTION ⇒ how many
OBJ–PL$_{\boxed{2}}$
are
LOCATION–MOD$_{\boxed{4}}$
	@$_{be39:ascription}$(be ∧
	  ⟨MOOD⟩int ∧
	  ⟨TENSE⟩$pres$ ∧
	  ⟨COP-RESTR⟩($\boxed{2}$ ∧
	    ⟨DELIMITATION⟩$variable$ ∧
	    ⟨QUANTIFICATION⟩$unspecific$) ∧
	  ⟨COP-SCOPE⟩($\boxed{4}$) ∧
	  ⟨SUBJECT⟩($\boxed{2}$ ∧
	    ⟨DELIMITATION⟩$variable$ ∧
	    ⟨QUANTIFICATION⟩$unspecific$) ∧
	  ⟨WH-RESTR⟩(h1:quantity ∧
	    howmany ∧
	    ⟨SCOPE⟩($\boxed{2}$ ∧
	    ⟨DELIMITATION⟩$variable$ ∧
	    ⟨QUANTIFICATION⟩$unspecific$)))

QUESTION ⇒ how many
OBJ–PL$_{\boxed{2}}$
are
there
	@$_{be1:presentational}$(be ∧
	  ⟨MOOD⟩int ∧
	  ⟨TENSE⟩$pres$ ∧
	  ⟨PRESENTED⟩($\boxed{2}$) ∧
	  ⟨SUBJECT⟩(there1:dummy ∧
	    there) ∧
	  ⟨WH-RESTR⟩(h1:quantity ∧
	    howmany ∧
	    ⟨SCOPE⟩($\boxed{2}$)))

QUESTION ⇒ do
you
follow
	@$_{follow1:action-motion}$(follow ∧
	  ⟨MOOD⟩int ∧
	  ⟨TENSE⟩$pres$ ∧
	  ⟨ACTOR⟩(you1:person ∧ **you** ∧
	    ⟨NUM⟩sg) ∧
	  ⟨SUBJECT⟩you1:person)

OBJ–SG–LC ⇒ one	@$_{c1:entity}$(context ∧
	  ⟨MODIFIER⟩(o1:number–cardinal ∧
	    one))

OBJ–SG–LC ⇒ x with $x \in$ {ball, box, book, chocolate, coffee, computer, cup, laptop, mug, object, pizza, place, screen, table, thing, couch, cube, column, closet, desk, tabletop, door, fax, floor, flower, needle, oven, phone, fridge, letter, jug, keyboard, mailbox, microwave, printer, block, bucket, chair, thread, tea, phone, tv, shelf, pin, game, star, triangle, square, car, circle, cylinder, cone, arm}	@$_{o6:thing}(y)$ with $y \in$ {ball, box, book, chocolate, coffee, computer, cup, laptop, mug, object, pizza, place, screen, table, thing, couch, cube, column, closet, desk, tabletop, door, fax, floor, flower, needle, oven, phone, fridge, letter, jug, keyboard, mailbox, microwave, printer, block, bucket, chair, thread, tea, phone, tv, shelf, pin, game, star, triangle, square, car, circle, cylinder, cone, arm}

OBJ–SG–LC $\Rightarrow$	chocolate bar	$@_{o11:thing}(\mathbf{bar} \wedge \langle \text{COMPOUND} \rangle (c1{:}e{-}substance \wedge \mathbf{chocolate}))$
OBJ–SG–LC $\Rightarrow$	corner	$@_{o12:e-region}(\mathbf{corner})$
OBJ–SG–LC $\Rightarrow$	place	$@_{o19:e-place}(\mathbf{place})$
OBJ–SG–LC $\Rightarrow$	top	$@_{o24:e-region}(\mathbf{top})$
OBJ–SG–LC $\Rightarrow$	side	$@_{o56:e-region}(\mathbf{side})$
OBJ–SG–LC $\Rightarrow$	colour game	$@_{o58:thing}(\mathbf{game} \wedge \langle \text{COMPOUND} \rangle (c1{:}entity \wedge \mathbf{color}))$
OBJ–SG–LC $\Rightarrow$	shape game	$@_{o59:thing}(\mathbf{game} \wedge \langle \text{COMPOUND} \rangle (c1{:}entity \wedge \mathbf{shape}))$
OBJ–PL–LC $\Rightarrow$ x with $x \in \{$balls, boxes, books, computers, cups, laptops, mugs, objects, screens, tables, things, cubes, columns, doors, needles, ovens, letters, jugs, blocks chairs, threads, pins, stars, triangles, squares, cars, circles$\}$		$@_{o58:thing}(y \wedge \langle \text{NUM} \rangle pl)$ with $y \in \{$balls, boxes, books, computers, cups, laptops, mugs, objects, screens, tables, things, cubes, columns, doors, needles, ovens, letters, jugs, blocks chairs, threads, pins, stars, triangles, squares, cars, circles$\}$
OBJ–PL–LC $\Rightarrow$	corners	$@_{o62:e-region}(\mathbf{corner} \wedge \langle \text{NUM} \rangle pl)$
OBJ–PL–LC $\Rightarrow$	places	$@_{o68:e-place}(\mathbf{place} \wedge \langle \text{NUM} \rangle pl)$
OBJ–PL–LC $\Rightarrow$	robots	$@_{o69:animate}(\mathbf{robot} \wedge \langle \text{NUM} \rangle pl)$
OBJ–PL–LC $\Rightarrow$	sides	$@_{o84:e-region}(\mathbf{side} \wedge \langle \text{NUM} \rangle pl)$
DET–SG–LC $\Rightarrow$	your	$@(\langle \text{DELIMITATION} \rangle unique \wedge \langle \text{NUM} \rangle sg \wedge \langle \text{QUANTIFICATION} \rangle specific \wedge \langle \text{OWNER} \rangle (you1{:}entity \wedge \mathbf{you} \wedge \langle \text{NUM} \rangle sg))$
DET–SG–LC $\Rightarrow$	the	$@(\langle \text{DELIMITATION} \rangle unique \wedge \langle \text{QUANTIFICATION} \rangle specific \wedge \langle \text{NUM} \rangle sg)$
DET–SG–LC $\Rightarrow$	a	$@(\langle \text{DELIMITATION} \rangle existential \wedge \langle \text{QUANTIFICATION} \rangle specific \wedge \langle \text{NUM} \rangle sg)$

DEM–SG–PRONOUN $\Rightarrow$ it	$@_{d1:thing}(\mathbf{it} \wedge$ $\langle \text{NUM} \rangle sg)$
DEM–SG–PRONOUN $\Rightarrow$ this	$@_{d2:entity}(\mathbf{context} \wedge$ $\langle \text{DELIMITATION} \rangle unique \wedge$ $\langle \text{NUM} \rangle sg \wedge$ $\langle \text{PROXIMITY} \rangle proximal \wedge$ $\langle \text{QUANTIFICATION} \rangle specific)$
DEM–SG–PRONOUN $\Rightarrow$ that	$@_{d3:entity}(\mathbf{context} \wedge$ $\langle \text{DELIMITATION} \rangle unique \wedge$ $\langle \text{NUM} \rangle sg \wedge$ $\langle \text{PROXIMITY} \rangle distal \wedge$ $\langle \text{QUANTIFICATION} \rangle specific)$
DEM–SG–LC $\Rightarrow$ this	$@(\langle \text{DELIMITATION} \rangle unique \wedge$ $\langle \text{NUM} \rangle sg \wedge$ $\langle \text{PROXIMITY} \rangle proximal \wedge$ $\langle \text{QUANTIFICATION} \rangle specific)$
DEM–SG–LC $\Rightarrow$ that	$@(\langle \text{DELIMITATION} \rangle unique \wedge$ $\langle \text{NUM} \rangle sg \wedge$ $\langle \text{PROXIMITY} \rangle distal \wedge$ $\langle \text{QUANTIFICATION} \rangle specific)$
DET–PL–LC $\Rightarrow$ the	$@(\langle \text{DELIMITATION} \rangle unique \wedge$ $\langle \text{QUANTIFICATION} \rangle specific)$
DET–PL–LC $\Rightarrow$ two	$@(\langle \text{DELIMITATION} \rangle existential \wedge$ $\langle \text{NUM} \rangle pl \wedge$ $\langle \text{QUANTIFICATION} \rangle specific \wedge$ $\langle \text{MODIFIER} \rangle (n1:number-cardinal \wedge \mathbf{2}))$
DET–PL–LC $\Rightarrow$ several	$@(\langle \text{DELIMITATION} \rangle existential \wedge$ $\langle \text{NUM} \rangle pl \wedge$ $\langle \text{QUANTIFICATION} \rangle unspecific \wedge$ $\langle \text{MODIFIER} \rangle (s1:quantity \wedge \mathbf{several}))$
DET–PL–LC $\Rightarrow$ some	$@(\langle \text{DELIMITATION} \rangle existential \wedge$ $\langle \text{NUM} \rangle pl \wedge$ $\langle \text{QUANTIFICATION} \rangle unspecific)$
DET–PL–LC $\Rightarrow$ all	$@(\langle \text{DELIMITATION} \rangle existential \wedge$ $\langle \text{NUM} \rangle pl \wedge$ $\langle \text{QUANTIFICATION} \rangle unspecific \wedge$ $\langle \text{MODIFIER} \rangle (s1:quantity \wedge \mathbf{all}))$
DEM–PL–PRONOUN $\Rightarrow$ these	$@_{c1:entity}(\mathbf{context} \wedge$ $\langle \text{DELIMITATION} \rangle unique \wedge$ $\langle \text{NUM} \rangle pl \wedge$ $\langle \text{PROXIMITY} \rangle proximal \wedge$ $\langle \text{QUANTIFICATION} \rangle unspecific)$

DEM–PL–PRONOUN $\Rightarrow$	those	$@_{c1:\text{entity}}(\textbf{context} \wedge$ $\langle\text{DELIMITATION}\rangle unique \wedge$ $\langle\text{NUM}\rangle pl \wedge$ $\langle\text{PROXIMITY}\rangle distal \wedge$ $\langle\text{QUANTIFICATION}\rangle unspecific)$
DEM–PL–LC $\Rightarrow$	those	$@(\langle\text{DELIMITATION}\rangle unique \wedge$ $\langle\text{NUM}\rangle pl \wedge$ $\langle\text{PROXIMITY}\rangle distal \wedge$ $\langle\text{QUANTIFICATION}\rangle unspecific)$
DEM–PL–LC $\Rightarrow$	these	$@(\langle\text{DELIMITATION}\rangle unique \wedge$ $\langle\text{NUM}\rangle pl \wedge$ $\langle\text{PROXIMITY}\rangle proximal \wedge$ $\langle\text{QUANTIFICATION}\rangle unspecific)$
LOCATION–RESULT $\Rightarrow$	between OBJ$_{\boxed{2}}$ and OBJ$_{\boxed{4}}$	$@_{l1:\text{m-whereto}}(\textbf{between} \wedge$ $\langle\text{ANCHOR}\rangle(\text{a22:physical} \wedge \textbf{and} \wedge$ $\langle\text{NUM}\rangle pl \wedge$ $\langle\text{FIRST}\rangle(\boxed{2}) \wedge$ $\langle\text{NEXT}\rangle(\boxed{4})))$
LOCATION–RESULT $\Rightarrow$	LOC–PREP–LC$_{\boxed{1}}$ OBJ$_{\boxed{2}}$	$@_{l2:\text{m-whereto}}($ $\boxed{1} \wedge$ $\langle\text{ANCHOR}\rangle(\boxed{2}))$
LOCATION–RESULT $\Rightarrow$	LOC–PREP–LC$_{\boxed{1}}$ PERSON–LC$_{\boxed{2}}$	$@_{l3:\text{m-whereto}}($ $\boxed{1} \wedge$ $\langle\text{ANCHOR}\rangle(\boxed{2}))$
LOCATION–RESULT $\Rightarrow$	LOCATION–LC$_{\boxed{1}}$	$@_{l4:\text{m-whereto}}(\boxed{1})$
LOCATION–RESULT $\Rightarrow$	from OBJ$_{\boxed{2}}$	$@_{l5:\text{m-wherefrom}}(\textbf{from} \wedge$ $\langle\text{ANCHOR}\rangle(\boxed{2}))$
LOCATION–RESULT $\Rightarrow$	out of OBJ$_{\boxed{3}}$	$@_{l6:\text{m-wherefrom}}(\textbf{out} \wedge$ $\langle\text{ANCHOR}\rangle(\boxed{3}))$
LOCATION–RESULT $\Rightarrow$	to the left of OBJ$_{\boxed{5}}$	$@_{l10:\text{m-whereto}}(\textbf{to} \wedge$ $\langle\text{ANCHOR}\rangle(\text{l1:e-region} \wedge \textbf{left} \wedge$ $\langle\text{DELIMITATION}\rangle unique \wedge$ $\langle\text{NUM}\rangle sg \wedge$ $\langle\text{QUANTIFICATION}\rangle specific \wedge$ $\langle\text{OWNER}\rangle(\boxed{5})))$
LOCATION–RESULT $\Rightarrow$	to the right of OBJ$_{\boxed{5}}$	$@_{l11:\text{m-whereto}}(\textbf{to} \wedge$ $\langle\text{ANCHOR}\rangle(\text{l1:e-region} \wedge \textbf{right} \wedge$ $\langle\text{DELIMITATION}\rangle unique \wedge$ $\langle\text{NUM}\rangle sg \wedge$ $\langle\text{QUANTIFICATION}\rangle specific \wedge$ $\langle\text{OWNER}\rangle(\boxed{5})))$
LOCATION–RESULT $\Rightarrow$	to OBJ$_{\boxed{2}}$	$@_{l30:\text{m-whereto}}(\textbf{to} \wedge$ $\langle\text{ANCHOR}\rangle(\boxed{2}))$

LOCATION–RESULT $\Rightarrow$	up to OBJ$_{\boxed{3}}$	$@_{130:\text{m-whereto}}(\textbf{to} \wedge$ $\quad \langle\text{MODIFIER}\rangle(\text{up1:m-direction} \wedge \textbf{up}) \wedge$ $\quad \langle\text{ANCHOR}\rangle(\boxed{3}))$
LOCATION–RESULT $\Rightarrow$	into OBJ$_{\boxed{2}}$	$@_{112:\text{m-whereto}}(\textbf{into} \wedge$ $\quad \langle\text{ANCHOR}\rangle(\boxed{2}))$
LOCATION–RESULT $\Rightarrow$	onto OBJ$_{\boxed{2}}$	$@_{112:\text{m-whereto}}(\textbf{onto} \wedge$ $\quad \langle\text{ANCHOR}\rangle(\boxed{2}))$
LOCATION–RESULT $\Rightarrow$	x with $x \in \{\textbf{away}, \textbf{aside}, \textbf{down}, \textbf{back}\}$	$@_{122:\text{m-direction}}(y)$ with $x \in \{\textbf{away}, \textbf{aside}, \textbf{down}, \textbf{back}\}$
LOCATION–RESULT $\Rightarrow$	close to OBJ$_{\boxed{3}}$	$@_{128:\text{m-whereto}}(\textbf{close} \wedge$ $\quad \langle\text{ANCHOR}\rangle(\boxed{3}))$
LOCATION–RESULT $\Rightarrow$	next to OBJ$_{\boxed{3}}$	$@_{130:\text{m-whereto}}(\textbf{next} \wedge$ $\quad \langle\text{ANCHOR}\rangle(\boxed{3}))$
LOCATION–RESULT $\Rightarrow$	closer to OBJ$_{\boxed{3}}$	$@_{129:\text{m-whereto}}(\textbf{close} \wedge$ $\quad \langle\text{DEGREE}\rangle comparative \wedge$ $\quad \langle\text{ANCHOR}\rangle(\boxed{3}))$
LOCATION–MOD $\Rightarrow$	LOC–PREP–LC$_{\boxed{1}}$ OBJ$_{\boxed{2}}$	$@_{114:\text{m-location}}(\boxed{1} \wedge$ $\quad \langle\text{ANCHOR}\rangle(\boxed{2}))$
LOCATION–MOD $\Rightarrow$	on the left of OBJ$_{\boxed{5}}$	$@_{117:\text{m-location}}(\textbf{on} \wedge$ $\quad \langle\text{ANCHOR}\rangle(\text{l1:e-region} \wedge \textbf{left} \wedge$ $\quad \langle\text{DELIMITATION}\rangle unique \wedge$ $\quad \langle\text{NUM}\rangle sg \wedge$ $\quad \langle\text{QUANTIFICATION}\rangle specific \wedge$ $\quad \langle\text{OWNER}\rangle(\boxed{5})))$
LOCATION–MOD $\Rightarrow$	on the right of OBJ$_{\boxed{5}}$	$@_{118:\text{m-location}}(\textbf{on} \wedge$ $\quad \langle\text{ANCHOR}\rangle(\text{l1:e-region} \wedge \textbf{right} \wedge$ $\quad \langle\text{DELIMITATION}\rangle unique \wedge$ $\quad \langle\text{NUM}\rangle sg \wedge$ $\quad \langle\text{QUANTIFICATION}\rangle specific \wedge$ $\quad \langle\text{OWNER}\rangle(\boxed{5})))$
LOCATION–MOD $\Rightarrow$	to the left of OBJ$_{\boxed{5}}$	$@_{119:\text{m-location}}(\textbf{to} \wedge$ $\quad \langle\text{ANCHOR}\rangle(\text{l1:e-region} \wedge \textbf{left} \wedge$ $\quad \langle\text{DELIMITATION}\rangle unique \wedge$ $\quad \langle\text{NUM}\rangle sg \wedge$ $\quad \langle\text{QUANTIFICATION}\rangle specific \wedge$ $\quad \langle\text{OWNER}\rangle(\boxed{5})))$
LOCATION–MOD $\Rightarrow$	to the right of OBJ$_{\boxed{5}}$	$@_{120:\text{m-location}}(\textbf{to} \wedge$ $\quad \langle\text{ANCHOR}\rangle(\text{l1:e-region} \wedge \textbf{right} \wedge$ $\quad \langle\text{DELIMITATION}\rangle unique \wedge$ $\quad \langle\text{NUM}\rangle sg \wedge$ $\quad \langle\text{QUANTIFICATION}\rangle specific \wedge$ $\quad \langle\text{OWNER}\rangle(\boxed{5})))$
LOCATION–MOD $\Rightarrow$	LOCATION–LC$_{\boxed{1}}$	$@_{121:\text{m-location}}(\boxed{1})$

LOCATION–LC ⇒	to the right	@(to ∧ ⟨ANCHOR⟩(l1:e–region ∧ **right** ∧ ⟨DELIMITATION⟩$unique$ ∧ ⟨NUM⟩sg ∧ ⟨QUANTIFICATION⟩$specific$))
LOCATION–LC ⇒	to the left	@(to ∧ ⟨ANCHOR⟩(l1:e–region ∧ **left** ∧ ⟨DELIMITATION⟩$unique$ ∧ ⟨NUM⟩sg ∧ ⟨QUANTIFICATION⟩$specific$))
LOCATION–LC ⇒	to your left	@(to ∧ ⟨ANCHOR⟩(l1:e–region ∧ **left** ∧ ⟨DELIMITATION⟩$unique$ ∧ ⟨NUM⟩sg ∧ ⟨QUANTIFICATION⟩$specific$ ∧ ⟨OWNER⟩(i1:entity ∧ **you** ∧ ⟨NUM⟩sg)))
LOCATION–LC ⇒	to your right	@(to ∧ ⟨ANCHOR⟩(l1:e–region ∧ **right** ∧ ⟨DELIMITATION⟩$unique$ ∧ ⟨NUM⟩sg ∧ ⟨QUANTIFICATION⟩$specific$ ∧ ⟨OWNER⟩(i1:entity ∧ **your** ∧ ⟨NUM⟩sg)))
LOCATION–LC ⇒	here	@($context$ ∧ ⟨PROXIMITY⟩m–$proximal$)
LOCATION–LC ⇒	there	@($context$ ∧ ⟨PROXIMITY⟩m–$distal$)
LOC–PREP–LC ⇒	x with $x \in$ {above, behind, close to, in, inside, near, near to, next to, on, left of, right of, under, over, along, around, below, beside, by, down, outside, in front of}	@(y) with $y \in$ {above, behind, close to, in, inside, near, near to, next to, on, left of, right of, under, over, along, around, below, beside, by, down, outside, in front of}
QUALIFIER ⇒	ADJUNCT–LC$_{\boxed{1}}$	@($\boxed{1}$)
QUALIFIER ⇒	ADJUNCT–LC$_{\boxed{1}}$ and ADJUNCT–LC$_{\boxed{3}}$	@$_{\text{qual:quality}}$(**and** ∧ ⟨FIRST⟩($\boxed{1}$) ∧ ⟨NEXT⟩($\boxed{3}$))
QUALIFIER ⇒	DEGREE–ADV–LC$_{\boxed{1}}$ ADJUNCT–LC$_{\boxed{2}}$	@($\boxed{2}$ ∧ ⟨MODIFIER⟩($\boxed{1}$))
DEGREE–ADV–LC ⇒	also	@$_{\text{deg1:m-intensity}}$(**also**)
DEGREE–ADV–LC ⇒	too	@$_{\text{deg1:m-intensity}}$(**too**)
DEGREE–ADV–LC ⇒	very	@$_{\text{deg1:m-intensity}}$(**very**)

ADJUNCT–LC $\Rightarrow$ x with $x \in \{\text{white}, \text{black}, \text{blue}, \text{green},$ $\text{brown}, \text{red}, \text{yellow}\}$	$@_{\text{ad1:q-color}}(y)$ with $y \in \{\text{white}, \text{black}, \text{blue}, \text{green},$ $\text{brown}, \text{red}, \text{yellow}, \text{orange}, \text{purple}\}$
ADJUNCT–LC $\Rightarrow$ x with $x \in \{\text{open}, \text{closed}\}$	$@_{\text{ad8:q-physical}}(y)$ with $y \in \{\text{open}, \text{closed}\}$
ADJUNCT–LC $\Rightarrow$ x with $x \in \{\text{round}, \text{elongated}\}$	$@_{\text{ad9:q-shape}}(y)$ with $y \in \{\text{round}, \text{elongated}\}$
ADJUNCT–LC $\Rightarrow$ x with $x \in \{\text{big}, \text{small}\}$	$@_{\text{ad9:q-size}}(y)$ with $y \in \{\text{big}, \text{small}\}$
ADJUNCT–LC $\Rightarrow$ x with $x \in \{\text{on}, \text{off}, \text{full}, \text{empty}\}$	$@_{\text{ad10:q-state}}(y)$ with $y \in \{\text{on}, \text{off}, \text{full}, \text{empty}\}$
ADJUNCT–LC $\Rightarrow$ x with $x \in \{\text{left}, \text{right}, \text{far}, \text{top}\}$	$@_{\text{ad10:q-location}}(y)$ with $y \in \{\text{left}, \text{right}, \text{far}, \text{top}\}$
ADJUNCT–LC $\Rightarrow$ better	$@_{\text{ad21:q-attitude}}(\textbf{good} \land$ $\langle \text{DEGREE} \rangle comparative)$
ADJUNCT–LC $\Rightarrow$ x with $x \in \{\text{last}, \text{other}\}$	$@_{\text{ad9:q-position}}(y)$ with $y \in \{\text{last}, \text{other}\}$
EVALUATION $\Rightarrow$ CUEWORD–ATTITUDE$_{[1]}$	$@([1])$
EVALUATION $\Rightarrow$ CUEWORD–MARKER$_{[1]}$	$@([1])$
EVALUATION $\Rightarrow$ CUEWORD–MARKER$_{[1]}$ CUEWORD–MARKER$_{[2]}$	$@_{\text{list22:d-units}}(\textbf{list} \land$ $\langle \text{FIRST} \rangle([1]) \land$ $\langle \text{NEXT} \rangle([2]))$
EVALUATION $\Rightarrow$ DEM–SG–PRONOUN$_{[1]}$ is CUEWORD–ATTITUDE$_{[3]}$	$@_{\text{e1:ascription}}(\textbf{be} \land$ $\langle \text{MOOD} \rangle ind \land$ $\langle \text{TENSE} \rangle pres \land$ $\langle \text{COP-RESTR} \rangle([1]) \land$ $\langle \text{COP-SCOPE} \rangle([3]) \land$ $\langle \text{SUBJECT} \rangle([1]))$
EVALUATION $\Rightarrow$ thanks	$@_{\text{e4:communication}}(\textbf{thank} \land$ $\langle \text{MOOD} \rangle ind \land$ $\langle \text{TENSE} \rangle pres \land$ $\langle \text{ACTOR} \rangle(\text{s1:entity} \land \textbf{speaker} \land$ $\langle \text{NUM} \rangle sg) \land$ $\langle \text{RECIPIENT} \rangle(\text{a1:entity} \land \textbf{addressee}))$
CUEWORD–ATTITUDE $\Rightarrow$ x with $x \in \{\text{wrong}, \text{right}, \text{sure}, \text{great},$ $\text{correct}, \text{incorrect}, \text{wonderful}, \text{good},$ $\text{true}, \text{false}, \text{bad}, \text{sorry}\}$	$@_{\text{cu1:q-attitude}}(y)$ with $y \in \{\text{wrong}, \text{right}, \text{sure}, \text{great},$ $\text{correct}, \text{incorrect}, \text{wonderful}, \text{good},$ $\text{true}, \text{false}, \text{bad}, \text{sorry}\}$
CUEWORD–ATTITUDE $\Rightarrow$ very good	$@_{\text{cu6:q-attitude}}(\textbf{good} \land$ $\langle \text{MODIFIER} \rangle(\text{v1:m-intensity} \land \textbf{very}))$

CUEWORD–ATTITUDE $\Rightarrow$ fine	$@_{cu13:marker}(\textbf{fine})$
CUEWORD–MARKER $\Rightarrow$ x with $x \in \{$ok, okay, fine, yes, yeah, no, right, good, sorry, alright$\}$	$@_{cu11:marker}(y)$ with $y \in \{$**ok**, **okay**, **fine**, **yes**, **yeah**, **no**, **right**, **good**, **sorry**, **alright**$\}$
PERSON–LC $\Rightarrow$ me	$@_{p1:person}(\textbf{I} \wedge \langle \text{NUM} \rangle sg)$
PERSON–LC $\Rightarrow$ you	$@_{p2:person}(\textbf{you} \wedge \langle \text{NUM} \rangle sg)$
PERSON–LC $\Rightarrow$ robot	$@_{p3:animate}(\textbf{Robot})$
PERSON–LC $\Rightarrow$ pierre	$@_{p4:person}(\textbf{Pierre})$
PERSON–LC $\Rightarrow$ gj	$@_{p5:person}(\textbf{GJ})$

D References

Ades, A. and Steedman, M. (1982). On the order of words. *Linguistics and philosophy*, **4**(4), 517–558.

Adjukiewicz, K. (1935). Die syntaktische Konnexität. *Studia Philosophica*, **1**, 1–27.

Ailomaa, M. (2004). *Two Approaches to Robust Stochastic Parsing*. Master's thesis, École Polytechnique Fédérale de Lausanne.

Allen, J. and Perrault, C. R. (1980). Analyzing intention in utterances. *Artificial Intelligence*, **15**, 143–178.

Allen, J., Miller, B., Ringger, E., and Sikorski, T. (1996). A robust system for natural spoken dialogue. In *ACL'96: Proceedings of the 34th Annual Meeting of the Association for Computational Linguistics*, Santa Cruz, USA. Association for Computational Linguistics.

Allopenna, P., Magnuson, J., and Tanenhaus, M. (1998). Tracking the time course of spoken word recognition using eye movements: Evidence for continuous mapping models. *Journal of Memory and Language*, **38**(4), 419–439.

Altmann, G. and Steedman, M. (1988). Interaction with context during human sentence processing. *Cognition*, **30**(3), 191–238.

Altmann, G. T. and Kamide, Y. (2004). Now you see it, now you don't: Mediating the mapping between language and the visual world. In J. M. Henderson and F. Ferreira, editors, *The Interface of Language, Vision, and Action: Eye Movements and the Visual World*, pages 347–386. Psychology Press, New York.

Anderson, M. L. (2003). Embodied cognition: A field guide. *Artificial Intelligence*, **149**(1), 91–130.

Areces, C. and Blackburn, P. (2001). Bringing them all together. *Journal of Logic and Computation*, **11**(5), 657–669. Special Issue on Hybrid Logics. Areces, C. and Blackburn, P. (eds.).

Areces, C. and ten Cate, B. (2006). Hybrid logics. In P. Blackburn, F. Wolter, and J. van Benthem, editors, *Handbook of Modal Logics*. Elsevier.

Areces, C., Blackburn, P., and Marx, M. (2001). Hybrid logics: characterization, interpolation and complexity. *The Journal of Symbolic Logic*, **66**(3), 977–1010.

Arkin, R. C. (1998). *Behavior-Based Robotics*. The MIT Press.

Arnold, J. E., Fagnano, M., and Tanenhaus, M. K. (2003). Disfluencies signal theee, um, new information. *Journal of Psycholinguistic Research*, **32**(1), 25–36.

Asher, N. and Lascarides, A. (2003). *Logics of Conversation*. Cambridge University Press.

Aust, H., Oerder, M., Seide, F., and Steinbiss, V. (1995). The philips automatic train timetable information system. *Speech Communications*, **17**(3-4), 249–262.

Bachy, S., Dister, A., Michel Francard, G. G., Giroul, V., and Philippe Hambye, Anne-Catherine Simon, R. W. (2004). Conventions de transcription régissant les corpus de la banque de données valibel. Technical report, Université Catholique de Louvain.

Bailey, D., Chang, N., Feldman, J., and Narayanan, S. (1997). Modeling embodied lexical development. In *Proceedings of the 19th Cognitive Science Society Conference*, pages 84–89. Erlbaum.

Baldridge, J. and Kruijff, G.-J. M. (2002). Coupling CCG and hybrid logic dependency semantics. In *ACL'02: Proceedings of the 40th Annual Meeting of the Association for Computational Linguistics*, pages 319–326, Philadelphia, PA. Association for Computational Linguistics.

Baldridge, J. and Kruijff, G.-J. M. (2003). Multi-modal combinatory categorial grammmar. In *EACL'03: Proceedings of the 10th conference of the European chapter of the Association for Computational Linguistics*, Budapest, Hungary.

Bar-Hillel, Y. (1953). A quasi-arithmetical notation for syntactic description. *Language*, **29**, 47–58. Reprinted in Y. Bar-Hillel. (1964). *Language and Information: Selected Essays on their Theory and Application*, Addison-Wesley 1964, 61–74.

Barsalou, L. (1999). Perceptual symbol systems. *Behavioral & Brain Sciences*, **22**, 577–660.

Bear, J., Dowding, J., and Shriberg, E. (1992). Integrating multiple knowledge sources for the detection and correction of repairs in human-computer dialogue. In *Proceedings of the 30th Annual Meeting of the Association for Computational Linguistics (ACL'92)*.

Berthoz, A. (1997). *Le sens du mouvement*. Odile Jacob.

Bertrand, R. and Priego-Valverde, B. (2005). Le corpus d'interactions dilogiques: Présentation et perspectives. Technical report, LPL-CNRS, Université de Provence.

Blackburn, P. (2000). Representation, reasoning, and relational structures: a hybrid logic manifesto. *Logic Journal of the IGPL*, **8**(3), 339–625.

Blackburn, P., de Rijke, M., and Venema, Y. (2001). *Modal Logic*. Cambridge University Press.

Blanche-Benveniste, C., Bilger, M., Rouget, C., and van den Eynde, K. (1990). *Le francais parlé : Etudes grammaticales*. CNRS Editions, Paris.

Bod, R. (1999). Context-sensitive spoken dialogue processing with the dop model. *Natural Language Engineering*, **5**(4), 309–323.

Bonasso, R. P., Kortenkamp, D., Miller, D. P., and Slack, M. G. (1995). Experiences with an architecture for intelligent reactive agents. In *Proceedings of the Fourteenth International Joint Conference on Artificial Intelligence (IJCAI 95)*, Montréal, Québec.

Breazeal, C., Brooks, A., Gray, J., Hoffman, G., Kidd, C., Lee, H., Lieberman, J., Lockerd, A., and Mulanda, D. (2004). Humanoid robots as cooperative partners for people. *International Journal of Humanoid Robots*.

Brenner, M., Hawes, N., Kelleher, J., and Wyatt, J. (2007). Mediating between qualitative and quantitative representations for task-orientated human-robot interaction. In *Proc. of the Twentieth International Joint Conference on Artificial Intelligence (IJCAI)*, Hyderabad, India.

Brooks, R. A. (1986). A robust layered control system for a mobile robot. *IEEE Journal of Robotics and Automation*, **2**(1), 14–23.

Brooks, R. A. (1999). *Cambrian Intelligence*. MIT Press.

Carroll, J. and Briscoe, E. (1996). Robust parsing - a brief overview. In J. Carroll, editor, *Proceedings of the Workshop on Robust Parsing at the 8th European Summer School in Logic, Language and Information (ESSLLI'96)*.

Carroll, J. and Oepen, S. (2005). High efficiency realization for a wide-coverage unification grammar. In *Proceedings of the International Joint Conference on Natural Language Processing (IJCNLP'05)*, pages 165–176.

Carroll, J. A. (1983). An island parsing interpreter for the full augmented transition network formalism. In *Proceedings of the first conference on European chapter of the Association for Computational Linguistics*, pages 101–105, Morristown, NJ, USA. Association for Computational Linguistics.

Caselli, M. C., Casadio, P., and Bates, E. (2000). Lexical development in English and Italian. In *Language Development: The essential reading*, pages 76–110. Blackwell publishers.

Chai, J. Y. and Qu, S. (2005). A salience driven approach to robust input interpretation in multimodal conversational systems. In *Proceedings of Human Language Technology Conference and Conference on Empirical Methods in Natural Language Processing 2005*, pages 217–224, Vancouver, Canada. Association for Computational Linguistics.

Chanod, J.-P. (2000). Robust parsing and beyond. In G. van Noord and J. Juncqua, editors, *Robustness in Language Technology*. Kluwer.

Charniak, E. (2001). Immediate-head parsing for language models. In *ACL '01: Proceedings of the 39th Annual Meeting of the Association for Computational Linguistics*, pages 124–131, Morristown, NJ, USA. Association for Computational Linguistics.

Cholakov, K., Kordoni, V., and Zhang, Y. (2008). Towards domain-independent deep linguistic processing: Ensuring portability and reusability of lexicalised grammars. In *Proceedings of the workshop on Grammar Engineering Across Frameworks*. Coling 2008 Organizing Committee.

Chomsky, N. (1957). *Syntactic structures.* Mouton, Den Haag (The Netherlands).

Clark, A. (1999). Embodied, situated, and distributed cognition. In *A Companion to Cognitive Science*, pages 506–517. Blackwell Publishers.

Clark, H. H. and Fox (2002). Using uh and um in spontaneous speaking. *Cognition*, **84**(1), 73–111.

Clark, H. H. and Schaefer, E. F. (1989). Contributing to discourse. *Cognitive Science*, **13**, 259–294.

Clark, S. and Curran, J. R. (2003). Log-linear models for wide-coverage ccg parsing. In *Proceedings of the 2003 conference on Empirical methods in natural language processing*, pages 97–104, Morristown, NJ, USA. Association for Computational Linguistics.

Clark, S. and Curran, J. R. (2007). Wide-coverage efficient statistical parsing with ccg and log-linear models. *Computational Linguistics*, **33**(4), 493–552.

Cole, R. A. and Zue, V. (1997). Spoken language input. In R. A. Cole, J. Mariana, H. Uszkoreit, A. Zaenen, and V. Zue, editors, *Survey of the State of the Art in Human Language Technology*. Cambridge University Press, Cambridge.

Collins, M. (1997). Three generative, lexicalised models for statistical parsing. In *ACL-35: Proceedings of the 35th Annual Meeting of the Association for Computational Linguistics and Eighth Conference of the European Chapter of the Association for Computational Linguistics*, pages 16–23, Morristown, NJ, USA. Association for Computational Linguistics.

Collins, M. (2002). Discriminative training methods for hidden markov models: theory and experiments with perceptron algorithms. In *Proceedings of the Conference on Empirical Methods in Natural Language Processing (EMNLP)*, pages 1–8.

Collins, M. (2003). Head-driven statistical models for natural language parsing. *Computational Linguistics*, **29**(4), 589–637.

Collins, M. (2004). Parameter estimation for statistical parsing models: theory and practice of distribution-free methods. In *New developments in parsing technology*, pages 19–55. Kluwer Academic Publishers.

Collins, M. and Roark, B. (2004). Incremental parsing with the perceptron algorithm. In *ACL '04: Proceedings of the 42nd Annual Meeting of the Association for Computational Linguistics*, page 111, Morristown, NJ, USA. Association for Computational Linguistics.

Crocker, M. (1999). Mechanisms for sentence processing. In G. . Pickering, editor, *Language Processing*. Psychology Press.

Dahl, D. A., Bates, M., Brown, M., Fisher, W., Hunicke-Smith, K., Pallett, D., Pao, C., Rudnicky, A., and Shriberg, E. (1994). Expanding the scope of the ATIS task: the ATIS-3 corpus. In *HLT '94: Proceedings of the workshop on Human Language Technology*, pages 43–48, Morristown, NJ, USA. Association for Computational Linguistics.

de Saussure, F. (1949). *Cours de linguistique générale*. Payot, Paris, 4e edition. publié par Charles Bally et Albert Sechehaye avec la collaboration de Albert Riedlinger.

Dourish, P. (2001). *Where the Action Is: The Foundations of Embodied Interaction*. MIT Press.

Dowding, J., Moore, R., Andry, F., and Moran, D. (1994). Interleaving syntax and semantics in an efficient bottom-up parser. In *ACL-94: Proceedings of the 32nd Annual Meeting of the Association for Computational Linguistics*, pages 110–116. Association for Computational Linguistics.

Dowty, D. (1979). *Word Meaning and Montague Grammar*. Reidel, Dordrecht.

Fauconnier, G. and Turner, M. (2003). *The Way We Think: Conceptual Blending and the Mind's Hidden Complexities*. Perseus Publishing.

Fernández, R. and Ginzburg, J. (2002). A corpus study of non-sentential utterances in dialogue. *Traitement Automatique des Langues*, **43**(2), 12–43.

Fine, S. (1998). The hierarchical hidden markov model: Analysis and applications. *Machine Learning*, **32**(1), 41–62.

Frege, G. (1892). Über Begriff und Gegenstand. *Vierteljahresschrift für wissenschaftliche Philosophie*, **16**, 192–205.

Gabsdil, M. and Bos, J. (2003). Combining acoustic confidence scores with deep semantic analysis for clarification dialogues. In *Proceedings of the 5th International Workshop on Computational Semantics (IWCS-5*, pages 137–150.

Gavaldà, M. (2004). SOUP: a parser for real-world spontaneous speech. In *New developments in parsing technology*, pages 339–350. Kluwer Academic Publishers, Norwell, MA, USA.

Ginzburg, J. (2009). *Semantics for Conversation*. CSLI Publications, Stanford. forthcoming in 2009.

Goodrich, M. A. and Schultz, A. C. (2007). Human-robot interaction: a survey. *Foundations and Trends in Human-Computer Interaction*, **1**(3), 203–275.

Goodwin, C. (1996). Transparent vision. In E. Ochs, E. A. Schegloff, and S. A. Thompson, editors, *Interaction and grammar*. Cambridge University press, Cambridge.

Gorniak, P. and Roy, D. (2007). Situated language understanding as filtering perceived affordances. *Cognitive Science*, **31**(2), 197–231.

Grice, H. P. (1975). Logic and conversation. In P. Cole and J. L. Morgan, editors, *Speech Acts: Syntax and Semantics, Volume 3*, pages 41–58. Academic Press, New York.

Grosz, B. J. and Sidner, C. L. (1980). Plans for discourse. In P. R. Cohen, J. Morgan, and M. E. Pollack, editors, *Intentions in communication*, pages 417–444. MIT Press, Cambridge.

Grosz, B. J. and Sidner, C. L. (1986). Attention, intentions, and the structure of discourse. *Computational Linguistics*, **12**(3), 175–204.

Grosz, B. J., Weinstein, S., and Joshi, A. K. (1995). Centering: a framework for modeling the local coherence of discourse. *Computational Linguistics*, **21**(2), 203–225.

Gruenstein, A., Wang, C., and Seneff, S. (2005). Context-sensitive statistical language modeling. In *Proceedings of INTERSPEECH 2005*, pages 17–20.

Guénot, M.-L. (2006). *Eléments de grammaire du francais: pour une théorie descriptive et formelle de la langue*. Ph.D. thesis, Université de Provence.

Hawes, N., Zillich, M., and Wyatt, J. (2007a). BALT & CAST: Middleware for cognitive robotics. In *Proceedings of IEEE RO-MAN 2007*, pages 998 – 1003.

Hawes, N., Sloman, A., Wyatt, J., Zillich, M., Jacobsson, H., Kruijff, G.-J. M., Brenner, M., Berginc, G., and Skocaj, D. (2007b). Towards an integrated robot with multiple cognitive functions. In *AAAI*, pages 1548–1553. AAAI Press.

Hawes, N., Wyatt, J. L., Sloman, A., Sridharan, M., Dearden, R., Jacobsson, H., and Kruijff, G.-J. (2009a). Architecture and representations. In H. I. Christensen, A. Sloman, G.-J. M. Kruijff, and J. Wyatt, editors, *Cognitive Systems: Final report of the CoSy project*. MIT Press.

Hawes, N., Wyatt, J., Sloman, A., Sridharan, M., Kopicki, M., Hongeng, S., Calvert, I., Kruijff, G.-J., Jacobsson, H., Brenner, M., Skočaj, D., Vrečko, A., and Majer, N. (2009b). The playmate system. In H. I. Christensen, A. Sloman, G.-J. M. Kruijff, and J. Wyatt, editors, *Cognitive Systems: Final report of the CoSy project*. MIT Press.

He, Y. and Young, S. (2005). Semantic processing using the hidden vector state model. computer speech and language. *Computer Speech and Language*, **19**, 85–106.

Heidegger, M. (1927). *Sein und Zeit*. Max Niemeyer Verlag, Tübingen, 6th edition.

Hjelmslev, L. (1974). *Prolegomena zu einer Sprachtheorie*, volume 9 of *Linguistische Reihe*. Hueber, München.

Hoyt, F. and Baldridge, J. (2008). A logical basis for the D combinator and normal form constraints in combinatory categorial grammar. In *Proceedings of the 46th annual meeting of the Association for Computational Linguistics*, pages 326–334. Association for Computational Linguistics.

Hsiao, K.-Y. and Mavridis, N. (2003). Coupling perception and simulation: Steps towards conversational robotics. In *Proceedings of IEEE/RSJ International Conference on Intelligent Robots and Systems*, pages 928–933.

Jackson, E., Appelt, D., Bear, J., Moore, R., and Podlozny, A. (1991). A template matcher for robust nl interpretation. In *HLT '91: Proceedings of the workshop on Speech and Natural Language*, pages 190–194, Morristown, NJ, USA. Association for Computational Linguistics.

Jacobsson, H., Hawes, N., Kruijff, G.-J., and Wyatt, J. (2007). Crossmodal content binding in information-processing architectures. In *Symposium on Language and Robots*, Aveiro, Portugal.

Jacobsson, H., Hawes, N., Kruijff, G., and Wyatt, J. (2008). Crossmodal content binding in information-processing architectures. In *Proceedings of the 3rd ACM/IEEE International Conference on Human-Robot Interaction (HRI)*, Amsterdam, The Netherlands.

Jakobson, R. (1976). *Six leçons sur le son et le sens*. Éditions de Minuit, Paris. (préface de Claude Levi-Strauss).

Jurafsky, D. and Martin, J. H. (2008). *Speech and Language Processing: An Introduction to Natural Language Processing, Computational Linguistics and Speech Recognition*. Prentice Hall, second edition.

Jurafsky, D., Shribergt, E., Fox, B., and Curl, T. (1998). Lexical, prosodic, and syntactic cues for dialog acts. In *Proceedings of ACL/COLING-98 Workshop on Discourse Relations and Discourse Markers*, pages 114–120.

Kamp, H. and Reyle, U. (1993). *From Discourse to Logic: Introduction to Model-theoretic Semantics of Natural Language, Formal Logic and Discourse Representation Theory*. Springer Verlag.

Kawamori, M., Shimazu, A., and Kawabata, T. (1996). A phonological study on japanese discourse markers. In *Proceedings of the 11th Pacific Asia Conference on Language, Information and Computation*.

Kelleher, J. (2005). Integrating visual and linguistic salience for reference resolution. In N. Creaney, editor, *Proceedings of the 16th Irish conference on Artificial Intelligence and Cognitive Science (AICS-05)*, Portstewart, Northern Ireland.

Knoeferle, P. and Crocker, M. (2006). The coordinated interplay of scene, utterance, and world knowledge: evidence from eye tracking. *Cognitive Science*, **30**(3), 481–529.

Kruijff, G.-J. M. (2001). *A Categorial-Modal Logical Architecture of Informativity: Dependency Grammar Logic & Information Structure*. Ph.D. thesis, Faculty of Mathematics and Physics, Charles University, Prague, Czech Republic.

Kruijff, G.-J. M., Kelleher, J. D., and Hawes, N. (2006). Information fusion for visual reference resolution in dynamic situated dialogue. In E. Andre,

L. Dybkjaer, W. Minker, H. Neumann, and M. Weber, editors, *Perception and Interactive Technologies: International Tutorial and Research Workshop, PIT 2006*, volume 4021 of *Lecture Notes in Computer Science*, pages 117 – 128, Kloster Irsee, Germany. Springer Berlin / Heidelberg.

Kruijff, G.-J. M., Lison, P., Benjamin, T., Jacobsson, H., and Hawes, N. (2007). Incremental, multi-level processing for comprehending situated dialogue in human-robot interaction. In *Symposium on Language and Robots*, Aveiro, Portugal.

Kruijff, G.-J. M., Lison, P., Benjamin, T., Jacobsson, H., Zender, H., and Kruijff-Korbayova, I. (2009). Situated dialogue processing for human-robot interaction. In H. I. Christensen, A. Sloman, G.-J. M. Kruijff, and J. Wyatt, editors, *Cognitive Systems: Final report of the CoSy project*. MIT Press.

Lakoff, G. (1987). *Women, fire and dangerous things: what categories reveal about the mind*. University of Chicago Press, Chicago.

Lakoff, G. and Johnson, M. (1980). *Metaphors We Live By*. University of Chicago Press, Chicago.

Lakoff, G. and Johnson, M. (1999). *Philosophy in the Flesh*. Basic Books.

Lambek, J. (1958). The mathematics of sentence structure. *American Mathematical Monthly*, **65**, 154–170.

Landragin, F. (2006). Visual perception, language and gesture: A model for their understanding in multimodal dialogue systems. *Signal Processing*, **86**(12), 3578–3595.

Langley, P., Laird, J. E., and Rogers, S. (2005). Cognitive architectures: Research issues and challenges. Technical report, Institute for the Study of Learning and Expertise, Palo Alto, CA.

Lascarides, A. and Asher, N. (2007). Segmented discourse representation theory: Dynamic semantics with discourse structure. In H. Bunt and R. Muskens, editors, *Computing Meaning: Volume 3*. Kluwer Academic Publishers.

Lison, P. (2008). A salience-driven approach to speech recognition for human-robot interaction. In *Proceedings of the 13th ESSLLI student session*, Hamburg (Germany).

Lison, P. (2009). A method to improve the efficiency of deep parsers with incremental chart pruning. In *Proceedings of the ESSLLI Workshop on Parsing with Categorial Grammars*, Bordeaux, France.

Lison, P. and Kruijff, G.-J. M. (2008). Salience-driven contextual priming of speech recognition for human-robot interaction. In *Proceedings of the 18th European Conference on Artificial Intelligence*, Patras (Greece).

Mann, W. C. and Thompson, S. A. (1986). Rhetorical structure theory: Description and construction of text sructures. Technical report, Information Sciences Institute.

Mann, W. C., Matthiessen, C. M., and Thompson, S. A. (1992). Rhetorical structure theory and text analysis. In W. C. Mann and S. A. Thompson, editors, *Discourse Description: Diverse Linguistic Analyses of a Fund-Raising Text*, pages 39–78. John Benjamins, Amsterdam and Philadelphia.

Manning, C. and Schuetze, H. (1999). *Foundations of Statistical Natural Language Processing*. MIT Press.

McKelvie, D. (1998). The syntax of disfluency in spontaneous spoken language. Technical report, University of Edinburg. HCRC Technical Report, RP-95.

Mel'čuk, I. A. (1988). *Dependency Syntax : Theory and Practice*. State University of New York Press, Albany.

Merleau-Ponty, M. (1945). *Phénoménologie de la perception*. Éditions Gallimard.

Miller, S., Schwartz, R., Bobrow, R., and Ingria, R. (1994). Statistical language processing using hidden understanding models. In *HLT '94: Proceedings of the workshop on Human Language Technology*, pages 278–282, Morristown, NJ, USA. Association for Computational Linguistics.

Moens, M. and Steedman, M. (1988). Temporal ontology and temporal reference. *Computational Linguistics*, **14**(2), 15–28.

Montague, R. (1974). *Formal Philosophy*. Yale University Press.

Montague, R. (1988). The proper treatment of quantification in ordinary english. In J. Kulas, J. H. Fetzer, and T. L. Rankin, editors, *Philosophy, Language, and Artificial Intelligence: Resources for Processing Natural Language*, pages 141–162. Kluwer, Boston.

Moore, R., Dowding, J., Gawron, J. M., and Moran, D. (1995). Combining linguistic and statistical knowledge sources in natural-language processing for atis. In *ARPA Spoken Language Technology Workshop*.

Moore, R. K. (2007). Spoken language processing: piecing together the puzzle. *Speech Communication: Special Issue on Bridging the Gap Between Human and Automatic Speech Processing*, **49**, 418–435.

Murphy, R. R. (2000). *Introduction to AI Robotics*. The MIT Press.

Ney, H. (1991). Dynamic programming parsing for context-free grammars in continuous speech recognition. *IEEE Transactions on Signal Processing*, **39**(2), 336–340.

Nilsson, N. (1984). Shakey the robot. Technical report, SRI AI Center. SRI AI Center Technical Note.

Oepen, S. and Carroll, J. (2000). Ambiguity packing in constraint-based parsing: Practical results. In *Proceedings of the 6th Applied Natural Language Processing Conference (ANLP 2000)*, pages 162–169.

Peirce, C. S., Houser, N., and Kloesel, C. J. W. (1998). *The Essential Peirce: Selected Philosophical Writings (1867-1893)*. Indiana University Press.

Petitot, J., Varela, F., Pachoud, B., and Roy, J.-M. (2000). *Naturalizing Phenomenology*. Stanford University Press.

Pieraccini, R., Tzoukermann, E., Gorelov, Z., Levin, E., Lee, C.-H., and Gauvain, J.-L. (1992). Progress report on the Chronus system: ATIS benchmark results. In *HLT '91: Proceedings of the workshop on Speech and Natural Language*, pages 67–71, Morristown, NJ, USA. Association for Computational Linguistics.

Pineau, J., Montemerlo, M., Pollack, M., Roy, N., and Thrun, S. (2003). Towards robotic assistants in nursing homes: Challenges and results. *Robotics and Autonomous Systems*, **42**(3-4), 271–281.

Poesio, M. and Traum, D. R. (1997). Conversational actions and discourse situations. *Computational Intelligence*, **13**(3), 309–347.

Power, R. (1979). The organisation of purposeful dialogues. *Linguistics*, **17**, 105–152.

Purver, M., Ginzburg, J., and Healey, P. (2001). On the means for clarification in dialogue. In *Proceedings of the Second SIGdial Workshop on Discourse and Dialogue*, pages 1–10, Morristown, NJ, USA. Association for Computational Linguistics.

Qu, S. and Chai, J. (2007). An exploration of eye gaze in spoken language processing for multimodal conversational interfaces. In *Proceedings of the Conference of the North America Chapter of the Association of Computational Linguistics*, pages 284–291.

Raymond, R. G. and Mooney, J. (2006). Discriminative reranking for semantic parsing. In *Proceedings of the COLING/ACL on Main conference poster sessions*, pages 263–270, Morristown, NJ, USA. Association for Computational Linguistics.

Rosé, C. P. and Lavie, A. (2001). Balancing robustness and efficiency in unification-augmented context-free parsers for large practical applications. In G. van Noord and J.-C. Junqua, editors, *Robustness in Language and Speech Technology*. Kluwer Academic Press.

Roy, D. (2001). Situation-aware spoken language processing. In *Royal Institute of Acoustics Workshop on Innovation in Speech Processing*, Stratford-upon-Avon, England.

Roy, D. (2005). Semiotic schemas: A framework for grounding language in action and perception. *Artificial Intelligence*, **167**(1-2), 170–205.

Roy, D. and Mukherjee, N. (2005). Towards situated speech understanding: visual context priming of language models. *Computer Speech & Language*, **19**(2), 227–248.

Roy, D. and Reiter, E. (2005). Connecting language to the world. *Artificial Intelligence*, **167**(1-2), 1–12.

Sacks, H., Schegloff, E. A., and Jefferson, G. (1974). A simplest systematics for the organization of turn-taking for conversation. *Language*, **50**(4), 696–735.

Searle, J. R. (1975). Indirect speech acts. In P. Cole and J. L. Morgan, editors, *Speech Acts: Syntax and Semantics, Volume 3*, pages 59–82. Academic Press, New York.

Sgall, P., Hajičová, E., and Panevová, J. (1986). *The Meaning of the Sentence and Its Semantic and Pragmatic Aspects*. Reidel Publishing Company, Dordrecht.

Sheridan, T. B. (1992). *Telerobotics, Automation, and Human Supervisory Control*. MIT Press.

Shriberg, E. (1996). Disfluencies in switchboard. In *Proceedings of ICSLP '96*, volume supplement, Philadelphia, PA.

Sima'an, K. (2004). Robust data oriented spoken language understanding. In *New developments in parsing technology*, pages 323–338. Kluwer Academic Publishers, Norwell, MA, USA.

Sjö, K., López, D. G., Paul, C., Jensfelt, P., and Kragic, D. (2008). Object search and localization for an indoor mobile robot. *Journal of Computing and Information Technology*. accepted.

Skočaj, D., Berginc, G., Ridge, B., Štimec, A., Jogan, M., Vanek, O., Leonardis, A., Hutter, M., and Hewes, N. (2007). A system for continuous learning of visual concepts. In *International Conference on Computer Vision Systems ICVS 2007*, Bielefeld, Germany.

Staab, S. (1995). GLR parsing of word lattices using a beam search method. In *Proceedings of Eurospeech'95*, Madrid, Spain.

Staudte, M. and Crocker, M. (2008). The utility of gaze in spoken human-robot interaction. In *Proceedings of Metrics for Human-Robot Interaction, Workshop at ACM/IEEE HRI 2008, Amsterdam, 12 March 2008*.

Steedman, M. (2000). *The Syntactic Process*. The MIT Press, Cambridge MA.

Steedman, M. and Baldridge, J. (2009). Combinatory categorial grammar. In R. Borsley and K. Börjars, editors, *Nontransformational Syntax: A Guide to Current Models*. Blackwell, Oxford.

Steedman, M. J. (1989). Constituency and coordination in a combinatory grammar. In M. R. Baltin and A. S. Kroch, editors, *Alternative Conceptions of Phrase Structure*, pages 201–231. University of Chicago, Chicago.

Steels, L. (1994). The artificial life roots of artificial intelligence. *Artificial Life*, **1**(1-2), 75–110.

Swerts, M., Wichmann, A., and Beun, R. (1996). Filled pauses as markers of discourse structure. In *Proceedings of ICSLP'1996*.

Tanenhaus, M., Spivey-Knowlton, M., Eberhard, K., and Sedivy, J. (1995). Integration of visual and linguistic information in spoken language comprehension. *Science*, **268**, 1632–1634.

Tesnière, L. (1959). *Éléments de syntaxe structurale*. Klincksieck, 2e édition.

Thomaz, A. L. (2006). *Socially Guided Machine Learning*. Ph.D. thesis, MIT.

Tomasello, M., Carpenter, M., Call, J., Behne, T., and Moll, H. (2005). Understanding and sharing intentions: The origins of cultural cognition. *Behavioral and Brain Sciences*, **28**, 675–691.

Tomita, M. (1986). An efficient word lattice parsing algorithm for continuous speech recognition. *Acoustics, Speech, and Signal Processing, IEEE International Conference on ICASSP '86.*, **11**, 1569–1572.

Traum, D. R. (1993). Rhetorical relations, action and intentionality in conversation. In *Proceedings of the ACL SIG Workshop on Intentionality and Structure in Discourse Relations*, pages 132–135.

van Benthem, J. (1997). Content versus wrapping: an essay in semantic complexity. In *Arrow logic and multi-modal logic*, pages 203–219. Center for the Study of Language and Information, Stanford, CA, USA.

Van Berkum, J. (2004). Sentence comprehension in a wider discourse: Can we use ERPs to keep track of things? In M. Carreiras and C. C. Jr., editors, *The on-line study of sentence comprehension: Eyetracking, ERPs and beyond*, pages 229–270. Psychology Press, New York NY.

Van Berkum, J., Zwitserlood, P., Brown, C., and Hagoort, P. (2003). When and how do listeners relate a sentence to the wider discourse? evidence from the n400 effect. *Cognitive Brain Research*, **17**, 701–718.

Van Berkum, J., Brown, C., Zwitserlood, P., Kooijman, V., and Hagoort, P. (2005). Anticipating upcoming words in discourse: Evidence from ERPs and reading times. *Journal of Experimental Psychology: Learning, Memory, & Cognition*, **31**(3), 443–467.

van Noord, G., Bouma, G., Koeling, R., and Nederhof, M.-J. (1999). Robust grammatical analysis for spoken dialogue systems. *Journal of Natural Language Engineering*.

Vapnik, V. (1998). *Statistical Learning Theory*. Wiley, New York.

Varela, F. J., Thompson, E., and Rosch, E. (1991). *The Embodied Mind: cognitive science and human experience*. MIT Press.

Vendler, Z. (1967). Verbs and times. In *Linguistics in Philosophy*, pages 97–121. Cornell University Press, Ithaca.

Ward, W. (1989). Understanding spontaneous speech. In *HLT '89: Proceedings of the workshop on Speech and Natural Language*, pages 137–141, Morristown, NJ, USA. Association for Computational Linguistics.

Weilhammer, K., Stuttle, M. N., and Young, S. (2006). Bootstrapping language models for dialogue systems. In *Proceedings of INTERSPEECH 2006*, Pittsburgh, PA.

White, M. (2006). Efficient realization of coordinate structures in combinatory categorial grammar. *Research on Language and Computation*, **4**(1), 39–75.

Wiggers, P. (2008). *Modelling Context in Automatic Speech Recognition*. Ph.D. thesis, Technische Universiteit Delft.

Wilson, M. (2002). Six views of embodied cognition. *Psychonomic Bulletin & Review*, **9**(4), 625–636.

Winograd, T. A. (1976). Towards a procedural understanding of semantics. *Revue Internationale de Philosophie*, **26**, 260–303.

Wittenburg, K. (1987). Predictive combinators: a method for efficient processing of combinatory categorial grammars. In *Proceedings of the 25th annual meeting of the Association for Computational Linguistics*, pages 73–80, Morristown, NJ, USA. Association for Computational Linguistics.

Zender, H. and Kruijff, G.-J. M. (2007). Towards generating referring expressions in a mobile robot scenario. In *Language and Robots: Proceedings of the Symposium*, pages 101–106, Aveiro, Portugal.

Zender, H., Mozos, O. M., Jensfelt, P., Kruijff, G.-J. M., and Burgard, W. (2008). Conceptual spatial representations for indoor mobile robots. *Robotics and Autonomous Systems*, **56**(6), 493–502.

Zettlemoyer, L. and Collins, M. (2007). Online learning of relaxed CCG grammars for parsing to logical form. In *Proceedings of the 2007 Joint Conference on Empirical Methods in Natural Language Processing and Computational Natural Language Learning (EMNLP-CoNLL)*, pages 678–687.

Zettlemoyer, L. S. and Collins, M. (2005). Learning to map sentences to logical form: Structured classification with probabilistic categorial grammars. In *UAI '05, Proceedings of the 21st Conference in Uncertainty in Artificial Intelligence, July 2005*, pages 658–666.

Zhang, Y., Kordoni, V., and Fitzgerald, E. (2007). Partial parse selection for robust deep processing. In *Proceedings of ACL 2007 (Association for Computational Linguistics), Workshop on Deep Linguistic Processing, Prague June 28, 2007*, pages 128–135.

Index

affordances, 13
ambiguities, 87
ambiguity, 3
architectural schema, 44
automatic speech recognition, 3, 63

back-channels, 22
behaviour-based robotics, 9
bi-directional coupling, 26
binding, 46
binding monitor, 46

cache, 52
Categorial Grammar, 29
chart scoring, 89
clarification request, 4
class-based model, 69
cognitive systems, 12
Cognitive Systems Architecture Schema, 44
Combinatory Categorial Grammar, 30
combinatory rules, 30
common ground, 26
confidence scores, 89
Context Change Potential, 39
context-free grammar, 131
context-sensitive language model, 63

context-sensitive lexical retrieval, 56
context-sensitive speech recognition, 5
context-sensitivity, 6
contextual features, 88
contextually activated words, 88
corrections, 22
cross-modal statistical model, 66

decision tree, 58
decoding, 84
derivational history, 87
dialogue move, 52
dialogue move interpretation, 58
discourse markers, 3
discourse reference resolution, 58
Discourse Representation Theory, 39
discourse-level composition rules, 77
discriminative model, 5
disfluencies, 2
distribution-free methods, 81
domain-specific grammar, 68
dynamic semantics, 39

early update, 91
error-correction rules, 78
event structure, 41
event structure recognition, 58

exact-match, 99
extra-grammaticality, 4

features of the discriminative model, 84

graceful degradation, 3
grammar relaxation, 5, 74, 75
grammatical analysis, 7
grounding, 10, 46

Hidden Markov Models, 7
hidden-variable problem, 83
hierarchical/linear recency, 65
human cognition, 25
human language processing, 10
human-robot interaction, 8
hybrid approach, 6
Hybrid logic, 32
Hybrid Logic Dependency Semantics, 32, 48
hybrid modal logic, 32

Incremental syntactic parsing, 56
incrementality, 27
information fusion, 47
integration, 6
intentionality, 26

language acquisition, 26
language model, 67
lexical activation network, 67
lexicon, 30
likelihood score, 74
linear model, 80
linguistic salience, 65
logical forms, 56

Max-margin classifier, 92
maximum-likelihood estimation, 81

modal logic, 32

nominals, 32
non-sentential utterances, 3, 22
non-standard CCG rules, 75
nucleus, 41, 52

object manipulation, 13
ontology-based mediation, 58

packed logical form, 51
packing of logical forms, 56
paradigmatic heap, 23
parallelism, 27
parameter estimation, 80
parametric models, 81
parse selection, 56, 74, 80
partial-match, 99
pauses, 20
perceptron, 83
plug-in nominals, 132
pragmatics, 28
proxy, 47

repetitions, 20
rhetorical relations, 40, 52
robust parsing of spoken inputs, 73

salience, 64
salience model, 5, 59, 63
satisfaction operator, 33
scenarios, 13
Segmented Discourse Representation Theory, 39
semantic features, 86
sense-plan-act, 9
service robots, 1, 11
shallow parsing, 7, 73
situated context, 10, 13
situated spoken dialogue, 8

situation awareness, 28
spatial understanding, 14
speech overlaps, 22
speech recognition features, 88
speech repairs, 22
stochastic context-free grammar, 82
stochastic parsing, 7, 73
structured classification, 80
Support Vector Machine, 92

syntactic features, 87

trigram language model, 69
type-shifting rules, 75

visual salience, 65

Wizard-of-Oz experiments, 69, 97
Word error rate, 99
word lattices, 48, 55